The Quotable Lover

The Quotable Lover

Edited by
Nancy Butler

THE LYONS PRESS
Guilford, Connecticut
An imprint of The Globe Pequot Press

To
my mother and father,
Doris and John Hajeski,
married 55 years and going strong …

Contents

Introduction

Love was before the light began,
When light if over, love shall be.
—THE THOUSAND AND ONE NIGHTS

From the dawn of time, love has been in the air—and depending on your own interpretation, it was the love of Adam for Eve or the love of one paramecium for another. The urge to merge has given all creatures a healthy regard for the procreative act, but only humans have overlaid this basic programming with a layer of deep emotional attachment—and glorified it with songs, poetry, and literature.

Love has been inspiring men and women since before the written word existed. Oral tradition is full of love ballads and sagas that tell of brave heroes rescuing fair damsels from unimaginable peril. The Bible offers us the sensual Song of Solomon and the inspiring story of Ruth, as well as the less happy romances of David and Bathsheba and Samson and Delilah. Greek and Roman mythology is rife with love-tossed gods prey to jealousy, manipulation, and hopeless infatuation. A powerful (if somewhat unfaithful) alpha couple headed each pantheon—Zeus and Hera for the Greeks; Jupiter and Juno for the Romans.

In the Middles Ages Eleanor of Aquitaine is credited with forming the Court of Love, which originated the notion of chivalry—that the knight *parfait* defended and honored women of all ranks. This gave rise to the troubadour, whose songs elevated courtly love to nearly unattainable heights. Centuries later the Elizabethans still craved love themes and found their appetites fed by the sonnets and plays of William Shakespeare.

In the late eighteenth century, the revolutionary philosophies of Jean Jacques Rousseau swept Europe, beckoning the world to revel in all things natural—and naturally this gave rise to an entire Romantic movement, which continued into the next century. Writers such as Lord Byron, Percy Shelley, Robert Burns, and Sir Walter Scott rebelled against the intellectual snobberies of Classicism and the constraints of Rationalism, while novelist Jane Austen, that astute observer of her class, gave us a surprisingly modern look at the foibles of love in her charming comedies of manners.

In France, Victor Hugo claimed the right of the artist to determine both subject and treatment in his novels. Other exponents of French Romanticism included Alexandre Dumas, Georges Sand, and Alfred de Musset.

The Victorians, with portraits of their lovelorn queen always before them, steeped themselves in overblown romantic literature, much of it lost now, but such shining lights as the Brontë sisters and Charles Dickens are with us still.

As the nineteenth century waned, exploring the psychology of love became the literary trend, perhaps a natural response to the lush indulgences of the Victorian era. Henry James and D. H. Lawrence scrutinized all aspects of romantic love, often at the emotional expense of their characters. F. Scott Fitzgerald and Ernest Hemingway used love as a platform for the telling of broader tales. Margaret Mitchell, likewise, used the romantic travails of her Southern belle to reflect the conflicts of the Civil War.

Eventually two world wars and the stress of the Atomic Age took their toll, and literary love fell out of favor during the latter part of the twentieth century, replaced by themes of self-discovery and personal redemption. The antihero reigned supreme. Yet, at the core of much contemporary writing there remained a love story.

Now, as we enter a new millennium, literary romance is again in the air. (It never really left the airwaves, since love songs always topped the charts.) Bestseller lists consistently reflect the taste for love stories, which are often then turned into movies. Mass-market paperback romances outsell every other popular genre combined and the annual revenues are in the billions of dollars. Somebody out there likes romance.

So now it appears we have come full circle—back to the Garden of Eden, where woman tempts man and man has to make a decision. To cleave or to leave. As long as that question hangs in the balance, writers will continue to explore it and readers will clamor to discover the answer.

As a writer of romance novels, I have always been intrigued by this particular tension. Since my teens I have explored the literature of love, seeking explanations for why hero and heroine are attracted to each other, why they resist and then succumb. Is it merely passion that moves them or something deeper, more enduring? I've discovered there are as many answers as there are people who have loved. That's the beauty of love—it gives everyone a sure and individual insight, some serious, some sly, some outright comical.

The quotes I've collected here—even the humorous ones—resonate with truth. They are the voices of not only great writers and poets, but also scientists, philosophers, entertainers, sociologists, and psychologists. Love is truly democratic—it strikes everyone, if they are lucky. And to the last man and woman, they all have something to say about it.

—Nancy Butler

1

This Thing
Called Love

Everyone admits that love is wonderful and necessary, yet no one agrees on just what it is.
—DIANE ACKERMAN

How can we possibly place one definition on love? How can we find the exact words for that feeling of supreme connection? When it engulfs us, we are beyond mere descriptions, when it abandons us, we are too bereft to seek for words. This hasn't stopped the poets, writers, and wits of the world from attempting to distill the essence of love into a few clever lines. Nothing, except perhaps war, has offered a greater motivation for men and women to take up their pens.

Although some historians claim our current notion of "falling in love" is of fairly recent vintage, the ancient Greeks and Romans certainly accorded the emotion enormous respect and saw it as a useful tool for dramatic catharsis. If love was a foreign notion to them, then how do we explain Plato pronouncing it "a divine madness"? That sounds a lot like modern love to me.

Whether love is experienced in the past or present tense, it leaves an irrevocable mark on those it has touched. From that point on, in our souls spring a personal definition, unique and heartfelt. Sometimes frustration mingles with tenderness, at other times anger overrides passion, and often humor is the lover's only recourse. These are all facets of romantic love, that bright diamond we covet, if only to keep away the darkness of solitude.

LOVE, n. A temporary insanity curable by marriage or by removal of the patient from the influences under which he incurred the disorder. . . . It is sometimes fatal, but more frequently to the physician than to the patient.

> AMBROSE BIERCE
> THE DEVIL'S DICTIONARY (1911)

Love gives naught but itself and takes naught but from itself.
Love possesses not nor would it be possessed; for love is sufficient unto love.

> KAHLIL GIBRAN
> THE PROPHET (1923)

The love which consists in this, that two solitudes protect and limit and greet each other.

> RAINER MARIA RILKE (1875–1926)

The story of a love is not important—what is important is that one is capable of love. It is perhaps the only glimpse we are permitted of eternity.

HELEN HAYES (1900–1993)

Love is a great thing. It is not by chance that in all times and practically among all cultured peoples, love in the general sense and the love of a man for his wife are both called love. If love is often cruel or destructive, the reasons lie not in love itself, but in the inequality between people.

ANTON CHEKHOV
"NAUKA," *COMPLETE WORKS AND LETTERS IN THIRTY VOLUMES* (1980)

Love is the only sane and satisfactory answer to the problem of human existence.

ERICH FROMM
THE ART OF LOVING (1956)

There is something self-renewing about love. Like the goddesses of Greece, it is able to renew its virginity in a bath of forgetfulness.

THOMAS MOORE
CARE OF THE SOUL (1992)

Falling in love consists merely of uncorking the imagination and bottling the common sense.

HELEN ROWLAND
A GUIDE TO MEN (1922)

Love is everything it's cracked up to be. That's why people are so cynical about it.

ERICA JONG (B. 1942)

The lover knows much more about the absolute good and universal beauty than any logician or theologian, unless the latter, too, be lovers in disguise.

GEORGE SANTAYANA
THE LIFE OF REASON (1906)

When a man's in love, he at once makes a pedestal of the Ten Commandments and stands on the top of them with his arms akimbo. When a woman's in love she doesn't care two straws for Thou Shalt and Thou Shalt Not.

W. SOMERSET MAUGHAM
LADY FREDERICK (1907)

Neither a lofty degree of intelligence nor imagination nor both together go to the making of genius. Love, love, love, that is the soul of genius.

WOLFGANG AMADEUS MOZART (1756–1791)

The intellect is always fooled by the heart.

LA ROCHEFOUCAULD (1613–1680)

Falling in love means sharing the unknown with another soul, being willing to step together into the wisdom of uncertainty.

DEEPAK CHOPRA (B. 1947)

I have been falling from the rim of a great, high place, somewhere back in time, for many more years than I have lived in this life. And through all of those years, I have been falling toward you.

ROBERT JAMES WALLER
THE BRIDGES OF MADISON COUNTY (1992)

Gravitation can not be held responsible for people falling in love.

ALBERT EINSTEIN (1879–1955)

Love is a force. It is not a result; it is a cause. It is not a product; it produces. It is a power, like money or steam or electricity.

ANNE MORROW LINDBERGH
LOCKED ROOMS AND OPEN DOORS (1974)

Who would give a law to lovers? Love is unto itself a higher law.

BOETHIUS
THE CONSOLATION OF PHILOSOPHY (524)

Love is an energy which exists of itself. It is its own value.

THORNTON WILDER
TIME (FEBRUARY 1958)

One word frees us of all the weight and pain of life: that word is love.

SOPHOCLES (C. 496–406 B.C.)

Great love will never mortify;
The more it kills, the better you get.

GACE BRULÉ (C. 1170–1212)

All love shifts and changes. I don't know if you can be
wholeheartedly in love all the time.

JULIE ANDREWS (B. 1935)

Love makes the time pass. Time makes love pass.

FRENCH PROVERB

We love because it's the only true adventure.

NIKKI GIOVANNI
READER'S DIGEST (1982)

He has stumbled into love, and now he's stuck there. He's fairly used to not getting what he wants, and he's dealt with it, yet he can't help but wonder if that's only because he didn't want anything too badly.

ALICE HOFFMAN
PRACTICAL MAGIC (1995)

Love, though it expends itself in generosity and thoughtfulness, though it gives birth to visions and to great poetry, remains among the sharpest expressions of self-interest.

THORNTON WILDER, QUOTED BY EDMUND FULLER,
"THE NOTATION OF THE HEART,"
THE AMERICAN SCHOLAR READER (1960).

Where there is love there is life.

MOHANDAS GANDHI (1869–1948)

Love cures people, the ones who receive love and the ones who give it, too.

KARL A. MENNINGER
SPARKS (1973)

———•••———

Love has nothing to do with what you are expecting to get, it's what you are expected to give—which is everything.

ANONYMOUS

———•••———

Love is a perky elf dancing a merry little jig and then suddenly he turns on you with a miniature machine gun.

MATT GROENING
LOVE IS HELL (1985)

Love is feared: it dissolves society, it's unpopular, and it's very rare.

CHRISTINA STEAD
FOR LOVE ALONE (1944)

It is with true love as it is with ghosts; everyone talks about it, but few have seen it.

LA ROCHEFOUCAULD (1613–1680)

Love . . . is a quicksilver word; though you see plainly where it is, you have only to put your finger on it to find that it is not there but someplace else.

MORTON HUNT
THE NATURAL HISTORY OF LOVE (1959)

Love is the profoundest of secrets. Divulged, even to the beloved, it is no longer Love.

HENRY DAVID THOREAU
"LOVE" (1852)

There is only one happiness in life, to love and be loved.

GEORGES SAND (1804–1876)

Only love interests me, and I am only in contact with things that revolve around love.

MARC CHAGALL (1887–1985)

Love is no hot-house flower, but a wild plant, born of a wet night, born of an hour of sunshine; sprung from wild seed, blown along the road by a wild wind.

JOHN GALSWORTHY
THE MAN OF PROPERTY (1906)

To love and be loved is to feel the sun from both sides.

DAVID VISCOTT
HOW TO LIVE WITH ANOTHER PERSON (1974)

Be of love (a little) more careful than of anything.

E E CUMMINGS, QUOTED IN *NEWSWEEK* (DECEMBER 1984).

A loving heart is the truest wisdom.

CHARLES DICKENS (1812–1870)

Accept the things to which fate binds you, and love the people with whom fate brings you together, but do so with all your heart.

MARCUS AURELIUS (121–180)

Love is life. All, everything that I understand, I understand only because I love. Everything is, everything exists, only because I love. Everything is united by it alone.

LEO TOLSTOY
WAR AND PEACE (1869)

Bitterness imprisons life; love releases it. Bitterness paralyzes life; love empowers it. Bitterness sours life; love sweetens it. Bitterness sickens life; love heals it. Bitterness blinds life; love anoints its eyes.

> HARRY EMERSON FOSDICK
> *RIVERSIDE SERMONS* (1958)

Hatred paralyzes life; love releases it.
Hatred confuses life; love harmonizes it.
Hatred darkens life; love illumines it.

> MARTIN LUTHER KING, JR. (1929–1968)

Poet's food is love and fame.

> PERCY BYSSHE SHELLEY
> "AN EXHORTATION" (1820)

Love, like a chicken salad or restaurant hash, must be taken with blind faith or it loses its flavor.

HELEN ROWLAND (1875–1950)

Love is only the dessert of life. The minute you try to live on dessert, you get sick of it, and you can get sicker of love than you can of anything else in the world.

DOROTHEA DIX (1802–1887)

The hunger for love is much more difficult to remove than the hunger for bread.

MOTHER TERESA (1910–1997)

There is no spectacle on earth more appealing than that of a beautiful woman in the act of cooking dinner for someone she loves.

THOMAS WOLFE
OF TIME AND THE RIVER (1935)

There is only one terminal dignity—love.

HELEN HAYES (1900–1993)

Being deeply loved by someone gives you strength; loving someone deeply gives you courage.

LAO-TZU (C. 570–490 B.C.)

Love is what happens to men and women who don't know each other.

W. SOMERSET MAUGHAM (1874–1965)

We are all born for love. It is the principle of existence, and its only end.

BENJAMIN DISRAELI (1804–1881)

Love never fails.

1 CORINTHIANS 13:8

Joy to forgive and joy to be forgiven
Hang level in the balances of love.

RICHARD GARNETT (1835–1906)

Doubt thou the stars are fire,
Doubt that the sun doth move,
Doubt truth to be a liar,
But never doubt I love.

> WILLIAM SHAKESPEARE
> *HAMLET* (1603)

The lover is a monotheist who knows that other people worship different gods but cannot himself imagine that there could ever be other gods.

> THEODOR REIK
> *OF LOVE AND LUST* (1957)

Love releases us into the realm of divine imagination, where the soul is expanded and reminded of its unearthly cravings and needs.

> THOMAS MOORE
> *CARE OF THE SOUL* (1992)

Love finds a way.

ENGLISH PROVERB

———

True love always makes a man better, no matter what woman inspires it.

ALEXANDRE DUMAS, *FILS*
CAMILLE (1852)

———

Ah! when will this long weary day have end,
And lend me leave to come unto my love?

EDMUND SPENSER
EPITHALAMION (1595)

———

In love there are no vacations. . . . No such thing. Love has to be lived fully with its boredom and all that.

MARGUERITE DURAS
LES PETITS CHEVAUX DE TARQUINIA (1953)

Love is not just looking at each other, it's looking in the same direction.

> ANTOINE DE SAINT-EXUPÉRY
> *WIND, SAND AND STARS* (1939)

When two people love each other, they don't look at each other, they look in the same direction.

> GINGER ROGERS, QUOTED IN "I DON'T WANT TO LIVE WITHOUT
> LOVE," *PARADE* (MARCH 1987).

Love is a snowmobile racing across the tundra and then suddenly it flips over, pinning you underneath. At night, the ice weasels come.

> MATT GROENING
> *LOVE IS HELL* (1985)

The supreme happiness in life is the conviction that we are loved.

VICTOR HUGO
LES MISÉRABLES (1862)

Loving is not just caring deeply, it's, above all, understanding.

FRANÇOISE SAGAN
LE SOIR (1960)

Are we ever our own master when it comes to falling in love? And if we are in love, can we act as if we were not?

DENIS DIDEROT
JACK THE FATALIST AND HIS MASTER (1770)

Love is the lord and the slave of all!

GEORGE MACDONALD (1824–1905)

There was never any yet that could wholly escape love, and never shall there be any, never so long as beauty shall be, never so long as eyes can see.

LONGUS
DAPHNIS AND CHLOE (2ND CENTURY)

Ama me fideliter! Fidem meam noto: De corde totaliter Et ex mente tota, Sum presentialiter Absens in remota. Love me faithfully! See how I am faithful: with all my heart, and all my soul, I am with you, though I am far away.

ANONYMOUS
"OMNIA SOL TEMPERAT," *CARMINA BURANA,* (C. 12TH CENTURY)

And all for love, and nothing for reward.

EDMUND SPENSER
THE FAERIE QUEEN (1589)

2

When First We Loved

*Love begins with a smile, grows with a kiss,
and ends with a teardrop.*

ANONYMOUS

There is an irresistible charm to the early stages of romance, those heady days before cynicism and doubt creep in. This is a time of innocence . . . hopeful, giddy and sometimes a bit blind. No matter our ages, whenever we begin to fall in love we find ourselves acting like teenagers again, mooning about, irrational, divinely goopy, and sighing over every foolish reminder of the beloved.

Though the protocol of courtship has changed from era to era, the basic tactics have remained the same. As a wise woman once pronounced, "He chased me until I caught him." Flirtation is the chief tool of courtship, the process whereby lovers attempt to attract—and distract—the opposite sex. The fan was once a powerful weapon in the art of flirtation; these days it's more likely to be the coyly wielded cell phone.

Literature is full of young lovers, perhaps beginning with Adam and Eve (Eve being the first really cheap date, requiring only an apple and a few fig leaves). Romeo and Juliet loved not wisely but too well. Young Lydia Bennett was swept off her feet by the dashing and dastardly Wickham, while the more pragmatic sisters, Jane and Lizzie, prudently waited out more promising (if somewhat haughtier) beaux.

Dating has its own perils; we have "the rules," we have rituals, we even have palimony in some states. We ration out affection on a numerical system, discreet kisses on a first date, perhaps something more intimate by the third or fourth date. We keep a mental scorecard. We hanker after relationships, we crave commitment, and dating allows us to discover if the other person is worthy of our affections.

And whether we look back at courtship with fond wistfulness or a more jaded eye, no one ever forgets their first encounters with love.

The first symptom of love in a young man is timidity; in a girl boldness.

> VICTOR HUGO
> *LES MISÉRABLES* (1862)

He whom you love, your Idiot Boy.

> WILLIAM WORDSWORTH
> "THE IDIOT BOY" (1798)

A girl's loving adoration is stronger than society's disapproval.

> HONORÉ DE BALZAC
> *MODESTE MIGNON* (1834)

Men always want to be a woman's first love—women like to be a man's last romance.

> OSCAR WILDE (1854–1900)

The magic of our first love is our ignorance that it can ever end.

> BENJAMIN DISRAELI
> *HENRIETTA TEMPLE* (1837)

We always believe our first love is our last, and our last love our first.

> ANONYMOUS

First love is an astounding experience and if the object happens to be totally unworthy . . . it makes little difference to the intensity or the pain.

> ANGELA THIRKELL
> *CHEERFULNESS BREAKS IN* (1941)

We don't believe in rheumatism and true love until after the first attack.

MARIE VON EBNER-ESCHENBACH (1830–1916)

I'm glad it cannot happen twice, the fever of first love.

DAPHNE DU MAURIER
REBECCA (1938)

First love is only a little foolishness and a lot of curiosity.

GEORGE BERNARD SHAW
JOHN BULL'S OTHER ISLAND (1907)

I kissed my first girl and smoked my first cigarette on the same day. I haven't had time for tobacco since.

ARTURO TOSCANINI (1867–1957)

I married the first man I ever kissed. When I tell this to my children they just about throw up.

BARBARA BUSH (B. 1925)

Where people wish to attach, they should always be ignorant. To come with a well-informed mind, is to come with an inability to administering to the vanity of others.

JANE AUSTEN
NORTHANGER ABBEY (1818)

If he had no desire to sleep with Fiona, then of course there was no necessity to pretend that every single thing she said was interesting.

NICK HORNBY
ABOUT A BOY (1998)

———

There's the thing about girls. Every time they do something pretty, even if they're not much to look at, or even if they're sort of stupid, you fall in love with them and then you never know where the hell you are.

J. D. SALINGER
THE CATCHER IN THE RYE (1951)

———

I'm doubled over with passion,
A plague on all the girls of the parish!

DAFYDD AP GWILYM
PLYGU RHAG ILID YR YDWYF (C. 14TH CENTURY)

I do know that girls in their early twenties are easy and sweet. . . . They are easy, I think, because they are sweet, and they are sweet, I think, because they are dumb.

> JOSEPH HELLER
> *SOMETHING HAPPENED* (1974)

Personally, I think if a woman hasn't met the right man by the time she's 24, she may be lucky.

> DEBORAH KERR (B. 1921)

Everyone knows that dating in your thirties is not the happy-go-lucky free-for-all it was when you were twenty-two.

> HELEN FIELDING
> *BRIDGET JONES'S DIARY* (1996)

Whenever I date a guy, I think, is this the man I want my children to spend their weekends with?

RITA RUDNER (B. 1956)

I date this girl for two years—and then the nagging starts: "I wanna know your name."

MIKE BINDER (N. D.)

Employees make the best dates. You don't have to pick them up and they're always tax-deductible.

ANDY WARHOL
ANDY WARHOL'S EXPOSURES (1979)

The major achievement of the women's movement in the 1970s was the Dutch treat.

NORA EPHRON
HEARTBURN (1983)

A woman without a man cannot meet a man, any man
... without thinking, even if it's for half a second, *Perhaps
this is the man.*

DORIS LESSING
THE GOLDEN NOTEBOOK (1962)

I go from stool to stool in singles bars hoping to get lucky,
but there's never any gum under them.

EMO PHILIPS (B. 1956)

I require only three things of a man: He must be hand-
some, ruthless, and stupid.

DOROTHY PARKER, QUOTED IN *YOU MIGHT AS WELL LIVE*
(1970).

We all suffer from the preoccupation that there exists . . . in the loved one, perfection.

SIDNEY POITIER (B. 1925)

———

We come to love not by finding a perfect person, but by learning to see an imperfect person perfectly.

ANONYMOUS

———

Jake liked his women the way he liked his kiwi fruit: sweet yet tart, firm-fleshed yet yielding to the touch, and covered with short brown fuzzy hair.

GRETCHEN SCHMIDT, ENTRY IN SAN JOSE STATE BAD WRITING CONTEST (1989).

There's not much meat on her, but what there is, is choice.

SPENCER TRACY (1900–1967)

The average man is more interested in a woman who is interested in him than he is in a woman with beautiful legs.

MARLENE DIETRICH (1901–1992)

It's no good pretending that any relationship has a future if your record collections disagree violently or if your favorite films wouldn't even speak to each other if they met at a party.

NICK HORNBY
HIGH FIDELITY (1995)

Like everyone who is not in love, he thought one chose the person to be loved after endless deliberations and on the basis of particular qualities or advantages.

MARCEL PROUST
REMEMBRANCE OF THINGS PAST (1922)

Many a man has fallen in love with a girl in a light so dim he would not have chosen a suit by it.

MAURICE CHEVALIER
NEWS SUMMARIES (17 JULY 1955)

Who ever loved that loved not at first sight?

> CHRISTOPHER MARLOWE
> "HERO AND LEANDER" (1598)

The only true love is love at first sight; second sight dispels it.

> ISRAEL ZANGWILL (1864–1926)

It is not love, but lack of love, which is blind.

> GLENWAY WESCOTT
> *NEW YORK HERALD TRIBUNE* (DECEMBER 1965)

Love looks not with the eyes, but with the mind,
And therefore is winged Cupid painted blind.

> WILLIAM SHAKESPEARE
> *A MIDSUMMER NIGHT'S DREAM* (C. 1595)

You don't love a woman because she is beautiful, but she is beautiful because you love her.

ANONYMOUS

In a great romance, each person plays a part the other really likes.

ELIZABETH ASHLEY (B. 1939)

My love she is a kitten,
And my heart's a ball of string.

HENRY SAMBROOKE LEIGH (1837–1883)

You have to walk carefully in the beginning of love; the running across fields into your lover's arms can only come later when you're sure they won't laugh if you trip.

JONATHAN CARROLL
OUTSIDE THE DOG MUSEUM (1991)

Dancing is a wonderful training for girls; it's the first way you learn to guess what a man is going to do before he does it.

CHRISTOPHER MORLEY
KITTY FOYLE (1939)

Aren't you afraid that you will bore her? . . . If she can't dance with you for half an hour, how will she be able to dance with you for life?

HENRY JAMES
THE PORTRAIT OF A LADY (1881)

Faint heart never won fair lady.

W. S. GILBERT (1836–1911)

My heart is a lonely hunter that hunts on a lonely hill.

WILLIAM SHARP (FIONA MACLEOD) (1855–1905)

Man is the hunter, woman is his game.
The sleek and shining creature of the chase,
We hunt them for the beauty of their skins;
They love us for it, and we ride them down.

ALFRED, LORD TENNYSON
"THE PRINCESS" (1847)

If it is your time, love will track you down like a cruise missile.

LYNDA BARRY
BIG IDEAS (1983)

With the catching ends the pleasures of the chase.

ABRAHAM LINCOLN (1809–1865)

If you want to win her hand,
Let the maiden understand
That she's not the only pebble on the beach.

HARRY BRAISTED
"YOU'RE NOT THE ONLY PEBBLE ON THE BEACH" (19TH CENTURY)

———

To become Love, Friendship needs what Morality needs
to become Religion—the fire of emotion.

RICHARD GARNETT (1835–1906)

———

Courtship to marriage is as a very witty prologue to a
very dull play.

WILLIAM CONGREVE
THE OLD BACHELOR (1693)

I am not the type of woman who goes to bed with every man at all. But if I meet a man, and I go to bed with him the first night, those relationships last.

ZSA ZSA GABOR (B. 1919)

Had we but world enough and time,
This coyness, lady, were no crime.

ANDREW MARVELL
"TO HIS COY MISTRESS" (1681)

Long engagements give people the opportunity of finding out each other's character before marriage, which is never advisable.

OSCAR WILDE (1854–1900)

If it were not for the Presents, an Elopement would be
Preferable.

GEORGE ADE (1866–1944)

———•••———

Come live with me and be my love;
And we will all the pleasures prove.

CHRISTOPHER MARLOWE
"THE PASSIONATE SHEPHERD TO HIS LOVE" (1599)

Ah, love, let us be true
To one another!

      MATTHEW ARNOLD
      "DOVER BEACH" (1867)

***

Better to be courted and jilted
Than never to be courted at all.

      THOMAS CAMPBELL
      "THE JILTED NYMPH" (1843)

***

Nunc scio quit sit amor.
Now I know what love is.

      VIRGIL (70–19 B.C.)

3

Passion and Seduction

*Pursuit and seduction are
the essence of sexuality.
It's part of the sizzle.*
—CAMILLE PAGLIA

It's a simple equation—interest leads to affection, affection to passion, passion to love. It's possible to desire someone without loving them, but rare to love a person romantically without desiring them. Passion is the point where heart and body meld, until we find ourselves possessed and obsessed. Some blame hormones, others blame a culture bent on gratification. Still, passion is a longtime companion to our species, the bond that held couples together when monogamy became essential to early agrarian cultures. The Bible acknowledges it, as does the Koran. Passion separates us from the animal kingdom—the conviction that only this chosen being can satisfy us physically and that we alone can sate them.

Seduction is the dark side of passion, the need to bend another to our will. It is often played out as a sort of mutual tug o' war, one party drawing back while the other moves forward. Men are the traditional seducers, but women have more than a few sirens in their camp, from Jezebel and Judith in the Bible, to Mata Hari and Madonna in more modern times. It's interesting to note that while the male seducer gets called charmingly roguish names such as rake, libertine, playboy, and ladies' man, his female counterpart earns more pejorative terms—mantrap, jailbait, tramp, and vamp.

Seduction with the sole intent to deflower is never pretty. On the other hand, when it is used as a stepping-stone to true intimacy, there is a beauty and grandeur to it. That breathless moment just before capitulation is the mainstay of romantic fancy, and the slow, relentless dance leading up to it, when desire and love at last combine, continues to fascinate us.

If passion drives you, let reason hold the reins.

ANONYMOUS

We must act out passion before we can feel it.

JEAN-PAUL SARTRE (1905–1980)

Anyone can be passionate, but it takes real lovers to be silly.

ROSE FRANKEN (1895–1988)

Sex is the most fun you can have without smiling.

ANONYMOUS

It's okay to laugh in the bedroom so long as you don't point.

WILL DURST (B. 1954)

It is more fun contemplating someone else's navel than your own.

ARTHUR HOPPE (1925–2000)

A man should kiss his wife's navel every day.

NELL KIMBALL (1854–1934)

Anyone who's a great kisser I'm always interested in.

CHER (B. 1946)

Let him kiss me with the kisses of his mouth: for thy love is better than wine.

SONG OF SOLOMON 1:2

For it was not into my ear you whispered, but into my heart. It was not my lips you kissed, but my soul.

JUDY GARLAND (1922–1969)

———

Where do the noses go? I always wondered where the noses would go.

ERNEST HEMINGWAY
FOR WHOM THE BELL TOLLS (1940)

———

You should not take a fellow eight years old and make him swear to never kiss the girls.

ROBERT BROWNING (1812–1889)

But do you know what is it to wait five months for a kiss?

ALFRED DE MUSSET, IN A LETTER TO GEORGES SAND (1834).

What is a kiss? Why this, as some approve:
The sure, sweet cement, glue and lime of love.

ROBERT HERRICK
"A KISS" (1648)

A kiss is a lovely trick designed by nature to stop speech when words become superfluous.

INGRID BERGMAN (1915–1982)

Singing is sweet, but be sure of this,
Lips only sing when they cannot kiss.

JAMES THOMSON (1834–1882)

Love, I find, is like singing. Everybody can do enough to satisfy themselves, though it may not impress the neighbors as being very much.

ZORA NEALE HURSTON (1891–1960)

Music and women I cannot but give way to, whatever my business is.

SAMUEL PEPYS
DIARY (1659–1669)

Music is love in search of a word.

SIDNEY LANIER (1842–1881)

———

I hope that one or two immortal lyrics will come out of all this tumbling around.

LOUISE BOGAN, OF HER AFFAIR WITH THEODORE ROETHKE.

———

At the touch of love everyone becomes a poet.

PLATO (C. 427–347 B.C.)

———

One does not write a love story while making love.

COLETTE
LETTRES AU PETIT CORSAIRE (1963)

Love is the source of language, and also its destroyer.

WALLACE STEVENS
WALLACE STEVENS: A CELEBRATION (1980)

To write a good love letter, you ought to begin without knowing what you mean to say, and to finish without knowing what you have written.

JEAN JACQUES ROUSSEAU (1712–1778)

Fill your paper with the breathings of your heart . . .

> WILLIAM WORDSWORTH, IN A LETTER TO HIS WIFE, MARY (1812).

More than kisses, letters mingle souls.

> JOHN DONNE (1572–1631)

. . . your letters made me love you so much that I went dippy in the dome, cultivated bats in the belfry, not to mention an owl or two in the outhouse . . .

> MALCOLM LOWRY, TO SWEETHEART CAROL BROWN (1926).

The perfect love affair is one which is conducted entirely by post.

GEORGE BERNARD SHAW (1856–1950)

All really great lovers are articulate, and verbal seduction is the surest road to actual seduction.

> MARYA MANNES
> *MORE IN ANGER* (1958)

———

Speak low if you speak about love.

> WILLIAM SHAKESPEARE
> *MUCH ADO ABOUT NOTHING* (C. 1598)

———

The light that lies
In woman's eyes
Has been my heart's undoing.

> THOMAS MOORE
> "THE TIME I'VE LOST IN WOOING" (C. 1810)

He gave her a look you could have poured on a waffle.

RING LARDNER (1885–1933)

She gave me a smile I could feel in my hip pocket.

RAYMOND CHANDLER
FAREWELL, MY LOVELY (1940)

When she raises her eyelids, it's as if she were taking off her clothes.

COLETTE
CLAUDINE AND ANNIE (1903)

A wise woman never yields by appointment. It should always be an unforeseen happiness.

STENDHAL
DE L'AMOUR (1822)

ARDOR, n. The quality that distinguishes love without knowledge.

AMBROSE BIERCE
THE DEVIL'S DICTIONARY (1911)

When they made love, it was with a quiet madness. . . . She wanted to beg him for promises, but she settled for moonlight and rough caresses. He wanted to make her a pledge, but he settled for her warmth and generosity.

NORA ROBERTS
WITHOUT A TRACE (1990)

Men who never get carried away should be.

MALCOLM FORBES (1919–1990)

Her heart did actual flip flops; it beat too fast and then too slow, and if that didn't mean she had some sort of condition, she didn't know what did.

ALICE HOFFMAN
PRACTICAL MAGIC (1995)

Oh, moment of sweet peril, perilous sweet!
When woman joins herself to man.

EDWARD ROBERT BULWER-LYTTON
"THE WANDERER" (1858)

Women complain about sex more often than men. Their gripes fall into two major categories. 1.) Not enough. 2.) Too much.

ANN LANDERS
TRUTH IS STRANGER (1968)

There is nothing better for the spirit or the body than a love affair. It elevates the thoughts and flattens the stomachs.

BARBARA HOWAR
LAUGHING ALL THE WAY (1973)

Love is the same as like except you feel sexier.

JUDITH VIORST (B. 1931)

Want him to be more of a man? Try being more of a
woman!

COTY PERFUME AD

I once made love for an hour and fifteen minutes, but it was the night the clocks are set ahead.

GARRY SHANDLING (B. 1949)

Eros is the youngest of the gods. He is also the most tired.

NATALIE BARNEY (1876–1972)

She used to tell her friends that every woman needs at least three men: one for sex, one for money, and one for fun.

SHANA ALEXANDER, OF BESS MYERSON.

The fantasy of every Australian man is to have two women—one cleaning and the other dusting.

MAUREEN MURPHY (N.D.)

It's the good girls who keep the diaries; the bad girls never have the time.

TALLULAH BANKHEAD (1903–1968)

When women go wrong, men go right after them.

MAE WEST (1893–1980)

Oh, Lord, it is not the sins I have committed that I regret, but those which I've had no opportunity to commit.

GHALIB PRAYER (C. 1800)

Sara could commit adultery at one end and weep for her sins at the other, and enjoy both operations at once.

JOYCE CARY
THE HORSE'S MOUTH (1944)

What men call gallantry and gods adultery
Is much more common where the climate's sultry.

LORD BYRON (1788–1824)

———•••———

There are few who would not rather be taken in adultery than in provincialism.

ALDOUS HUXLEY
ANTIC HAY (1923)

———•••———

You know, of course, that the Tasmanians, who never committed adultery, are now extinct.

W. SOMERSET MAUGHAM
THE BREAD-WINNER (1930)

It seemed to Annie . . . that in what followed there was no element of choice. Some things simply were and could not be rendered otherwise. She trembled now at its doing and would tremble later at the thought of it, though never once with regret.

NICHOLAS EVANS
THE HORSE WHISPERER (1995)

If men knew all that women think, they'd be twenty times more daring.

ALPHONSE KARR (1808–1890)

Familiarity breeds attempt.

GOODMAN ACE (1899–1982)

Sexual behavior is often judged by clergymen whose qualifications include their solemn renunciation of sexual intercourse.

DAVID REUBEN, M.D.
EVERYTHING YOU EVER WANTED TO KNOW ABOUT SEX (1969)

Platonic love is love from the neck up.

THYRA SAMTER WINSLOW
NEWS SUMMARIES (AUGUST 1952)

I've been on more laps than a napkin.

MAE WEST (1893–1980)

I'm suggesting we call sex something else, and it should include everything from kissing to sitting close together.

SHERE HITE (B. 1943)

The omnipresent process of sex, as it is woven into the whole texture of our man's or woman's body, is the pattern of all the process of our life.

HAVELOCK ELLIS
THE NEW SPIRIT (1890)

The gate of the subtle and profound female
Is the root of Heaven and Earth.
It is continuous, and seems to be always existing.
Use it and you will never wear it out.

LAO-TZU
TAO TE CHING (550 B.C.)

Man's love is of man's life a thing apart,
'Tis women's whole existence.

LORD BYRON
DON JUAN (1818)

There is no fury like a woman searching for a new lover.

> CYRIL CONNOLLY
> *THE UNQUIET GRAVE* (1944)

Absence, that common cure of love.

> MIGUEL DE CERVANTES
> *DON QUIXOTE* (1605)

Absence is to love what wind is to fire; it extinguishes the small, it enkindles the great.

> COMTE DE BUSSY-RABUTIN
> *HISTOIRE AMOUREUSE DES GAULES* (1665)

Absence does not make the heart grow fonder. But it sure heats up the blood.

> ELIZABETH ASHLEY (B. 1941)

Love is a fire. But whether it is going to warm your hearth or burn down your house, you can never tell.

JOAN CRAWFORD (1906–1977)

Love [Emma] believed, had to come suddenly with great thunder-claps and lightning flashes—a storm from the heavens upon a life, turning it upside down, blowing away its pretty will like leaves, and carrying one's heart to the edge of the abyss.

GUSTAVE FLAUBERT
MADAME BOVARY (1857)

She had awakened something in me that had slumbered far too long. Not only did I feel passion again, I felt the return of hope.

PAT CONROY
THE PRINCE OF TIDES (1986)

"Let go of this"—the voice was hissing now—"it's out-running you."

But the slow, sweet tango had begun.

ROBERT JAMES WALLER
THE BRIDGES OF MADISON COUNTY (1992)

I learned nothing of diplomacy during those months. Instead I learned the art of rapture. I learned how to give it and how to receive it. I learned how much more it's worth when it's both given and received.

VONDA N. MCINTYRE
THE MOON AND THE SUN (1997)

We desire nothing so much as what we ought not to have.

PUBLILIUS SYRUS
MAXIM (C. 42 B.C.)

Is there anything better than to be longing for something, when you know it is within reach?

GRETA GARBO, QUOTED IN *THE DIVINE GARBO* (1979).

Love is an irresistible desire to be irresistibly desired.

ROBERT FROST (1874–1963)

Can one desire too much of a good thing?

WILLIAM SHAKESPEARE
AS YOU LIKE IT (C. 1599)

Pleasure's a sin, and sometimes sin's a pleasure.

LORD BYRON
DON JUAN (1818)

Christianity, by making love a sin, did love a great service.

ANATOLE FRANCE
THE GARDEN OF EPICURUS (1894)

———•••———

There are several good protections against temptation, but the surest is cowardice.

MARK TWAIN
FOLLOWING THE EQUATOR (1897)

———•••———

At 82, I feel like a 20-year-old but, unfortunately, there's never one around.

MILTON BERLE (1908–2002)

———•••———

When turkeys mate they think of swans.

JOHNNY CARSON (B. 1925)

After coition every animal is sad.
> LATIN MAXIM

God made coitus, man made love.
> E. AND J. DE GONCOURT
> JOURNAL (1891)

"Cogito ergo sum."—Descartes
"Coito ergo sum."—Freud
> MEN'S ROOM GRAFFITI, ADELPHI UNIVERSITY

As a psychiatrist I am constantly impressed with one outstanding paradox presented to me constantly. In virtually every patient, I see a person living in the Space Age who has left his (or her) sexual organs in the Stone Age.
> DAVID REUBEN, M.D.
> EVERYTHING YOU EVER WANTED TO KNOW ABOUT SEX (1969)

I don't mind where people make love, so long as they don't do it in the street and frighten the horses.

MRS. PATRICK CAMPBELL (1865–1940)

France is the only place where you can make love in the afternoon without people hammering on your door.

BARBARA CARTLAND, QUOTED IN THE GUARDIAN
(24 DECEMBER 1984).

The only reason I would take up jogging would be so I could hear heavy breathing again.

ERMA BOMBECK (1927–1996)

4

Love and Marriage

I know I weigh seventeen stone and my missus looks like a ninepenny rabbit, and yet we're as happy as can be.
—P. G. WODEHOUSE

Love and marriage . . . according to stand-up comics, this term is an oxymoron. They claim that as soon as the marriage license has been signed every manner of clichéd behavior begins, and love goes right out the window. Whether this is true or not—and the divorce rates in this country may bear it out—a great many couples do manage to make it work.

Marriage has always been in vogue. Whether to cement a dynasty, ensure continuation of a family name, or merely to appease physical desire, lovers have plighted their troth since the earliest days of recorded history. Nearly every culture, old or new, on every continent and archipelago, features a wedding ritual. Whether we are all equipped to withstand the day-to-day presence of "a beloved stranger" is another story.

Until quite recently divorce was not an easy option and many couples learned to make do. Upper-class men took mistresses, and it was not uncommon for a married lady to take a lover (once the need for an heir and a spare had been met). This practice gave rise to dramatic "bedroom farces," such as *The Marriage of Figaro,* with cheating couples darting in and out of bedrooms in a frenzy of hair-trigger timing. That audiences approved such goings-on leads us to believe that infidelities might be overlooked, if they involved the quest for true love—and providing they were funny.

It is a misconception that great artists and writers were by and large unwed. Art and marriage might be uneasy bedfellows, but a comfortable spouse gives the creative genius the luxury of time to create without having to bother with domestic details. And it wasn't all housekeeping; many artists fell in love with and married their favorite models; many writers courted and wed those who inspired them.

Despite all the wry commentary from the comedians, we have no reason to think marriage will fall out of favor with future generations. And perhaps they will learn, as couples from earlier eras did, that "when you go in expecting less, you sometimes end up getting more."

A lady's imagination is very rapid; it jumps from admiration to love, from love to matrimony in a moment.

JANE AUSTEN
PRIDE AND PREJUDICE (1813)

Love is not weakness. It is strong. Only the sacrament of marriage can contain it.

BORIS PASTERNAK
DR. ZHIVAGO (1957)

Always get married in the morning. That way, if it doesn't work out, you haven't wasted a whole day.

MICKEY ROONEY (B. 1920)

I know what I wish Ralph Nader would investigate next. Marriage. It's not safe—it's not safe at all.

JEAN KERR (B. 1923)

With this ring I thee wed, with my body I thee worship, and with all my worldly good I thee endow.

WEDDING VOW, BOOK OF COMMON PRAYER

Love, the strongest and deepest element in all life, the harbinger of hope, of joy, of ecstasy; love, the defier of all laws, of all conventions; love, the freest, the most powerful moulder of human destiny; how can such an all-compelling force be synonymous with that poor little State and Church-begotten weed, marriage?

EMMA GOLDMAN
ANARCHISM AND OTHER ESSAYS (1910)

When two people are under the influence of the most violent, most insane, most delusive, most transient of passions, they are required to swear that they will remain in that excited and exhausting condition continuously until death do them part.

GEORGE BERNARD SHAW (1856–1950)

One cardinal rule of marriage should never be forgotten: "Give little, give seldom, and above all, give grudgingly." Otherwise, what could have been a proper marriage could become an orgy of sexual lust.

RUTH SMYTHERS
MARRIAGE ADVICE FOR WOMEN (1894)

Marriage is the result of the longing for the deep, deep peace of the double bed after the hurley-burley of the chaise-longue.

MRS. PATRICK CAMPBELL (1865–1940)

Marriage is that relation between man and woman in which the independence is equal, the dependence mutual, and the obligation reciprocal.

LOUIS KAUFMAN ANSPACHER (1878–1947)

In married life three is company and two none.

OSCAR WILDE
THE IMPORTANCE OF BEING ERNEST (1895)

Marriage is a three-ring circus: engagement ring, wedding ring, and suffering.

ANONYMOUS

Ideally, couples need three lives; one for him, one for her, and one for them together.

JACQUELINE BISSET (B. 1944)

Marrying a man is like buying something you've been admiring for a long time in a shop window. You may love it when you get it home, but it doesn't always go with everything else.

JEAN KERR (B. 1923)

A husband is what's left of a lover, after the nerve has been extracted.

HELEN ROWLAND
A GUIDE TO MEN (1922)

It is easier to be a lover than a husband for the simple reason that it is more difficult to be witty every day than to say pretty things from time to time.

HONORÉ DE BALZAC
PHYSIOLOGIE DU MARIAGE (1829)

The best way to get husbands to do something is to suggest that perhaps they are too old to do it.

SHIRLEY MACLAINE (B. 1934)

The divine right of husbands, like the divine right of kings, may, it is hoped, in this enlightened age, be contested without danger.

MARY WOLLSTONECRAFT
A VINDICATION OF THE RIGHTS OF WOMEN (1792)

Whenever you want to marry someone, go have lunch
with his ex-wife.

SHELLEY WINTERS (B. 1922)

Marriage is a romance in which the hero dies in the first
chapter.

ANONYMOUS

I married beneath me. All women do.

LADY NANCY ASTOR (1879–1964)

The trouble with some women is that they get all excited
about nothing—and then marry him.

CHER (B. 1946)

Not all women are fools. Some are single.

BUMPER STICKER

＊＊＊＊＊

An archeologist is the best husband any woman can have:
The older she gets, that more interested he is in her.

AGATHA CHRISTIE (1890–1976)

I think men who have a pierced ear are better prepared for marriage. They've experienced pain and bought jewelry.

RITA RUDNER (B. 1956)

When he is late for dinner and I know he must be either having an affair or lying dead in the street, I always hope he's dead.

JUDITH VIORST (B. 1931)

Husbands are like fires. They go out if left unattended.

ZSA ZSA GABOR (B. 1919)

He's her future ex-husband.

ANONYMOUS

Someone once asked me why women don't gamble as much as men do and I gave the commonsensical reply that we don't have as much money. That was a true but incomplete answer. In fact, women's total instinct for gambling is satisfied by marriage.

GLORIA STEINEM (B. 1934)

Perfection is what American women expect to find in their husbands . . . but English women only hope to find it in their butlers.

W. SOMERSET MAUGHAM (1874–1965)

God help the man who won't marry until he finds a perfect woman, and God help him still more if he finds her.

BENJAMIN TILLETT (1860–1943)

Many a man in love with a dimple makes the mistake of marrying the whole girl.

STEPHEN LEACOCK (1869–1944)

Where one goes wrong when looking for the ideal girl is in making one's selection before walking the full length of the counter.

P. G. WODEHOUSE
MUCH OBLIGED, JEEVES (1971)

If men knew how women pass the time when they are alone, they'd never marry.

O. HENRY
THE FOUR MILLION (1906)

He that hath wife and children hath given hostages to fortune; for they are impediments to great enterprise, either of virtue or mischief.

FRANCIS BACON
"OF MARRIAGE AND SINGLE LIFE" (1601)

Variability is one of the virtues of a woman. It avoids the crude requirement of polygamy. So long as you have one good wife you are sure to have a spiritual harem.

> G. K. CHESTERTON
> *ALARMS AND DISCURSIONS* (1910)

There is trouble with a wife, but it's even worse with a woman who is not a wife.

> LEO TOLSTOY
> *ANNA KARENINA* (1876)

A successful man is one who makes more money than his wife can spend. A successful woman is one who can find such a man.

> LANA TURNER (1920–1995)

No man ever prospered in the world without the consent
and cooperation of his wife.

ABIGAIL ADAMS (1744–1818)

It's hard for women, you know.
To get away. There's always so much to do.
Husbands to be patted and put in good tempers;
Servants to be poked out; Children washed.

ARISTOPHANES
LYSISTRATA (411 B.C.)

A man's home is his wife's castle.

ALEXANDER CHASE
PERSPECTIVES (1966)

A man's home may seem to be his castle on the outside; inside it is more often his nursery.

CLARE BOOTH LUCE (1903–1987)

In the long run wives are to be paid in a peculiar coin— consideration for their feelings. As it usually turns out this is an enormous, unthinkable inflation few men will remit, or if they will, only with a sense of being over-charged.

ELIZABETH HARDWICK
SEDUCTION AND BETRAYAL (1974)

Every man who is high up loves to think he has done it all himself; and the wife smiles, and lets it go at that. It's our only joke. Every woman knows that.

J. M. BARRIE
WHAT EVERY WOMAN KNOWS (1908)

A man likes his wife to be just clever enough to appreci-
ate his cleverness, and just stupid enough to admire it.

ISRAEL ZANGWILL (1864–1926)

A man must marry only a very pretty woman in case he
should ever want some other man to take her off his
hands.

SACHA GUITRY (1885–1957)

If a wife . . . has persisted in going out, has acted the fool,
and wasted her house . . . her husband may divorce her,
or he may take another woman to wife and the first shall
live as a slave in her husband's house.

HAMMURABI'S CODE (C. 1780 B.C.)

A man who marries a woman to educate her falls a victim to the same fallacy as the woman who marries a man to reform him.

ELBERT HUBBARD (1856–1915)

Our house has never been anything but a playpen. I have been your doll wife, just as I was daddy's doll child.

HENRIK IBSEN
A DOLL'S HOUSE (1879)

When a woman gets married it's like jumping into a hole in the ice in the middle of winter; you do it once, and you remember it the rest of your days.

MAXIM GORKY
THE LOWER DEPTHS (1902)

Men are horribly tedious when they are good husbands, and abominably conceited when they are not.

OSCAR WILDE
A WOMAN OF NO IMPORTANCE (1893)

Faithful women are all alike. They think only of their fidelity and never of their husbands.

JEAN GIRAUDOUX
AMPHITRYON (1929)

Never be unfaithful to a lover, except with your wife.

P. J. O'ROURKE (B. 1947)

Elizabeth Taylor was asked how many husbands she's had. And she replied, "Mine or other people's?"

ANONYMOUS

When a man steals your wife, there is no better revenge than to let him keep her.

SACHA GUITRY
ELLES ET TOI (1948)

A lost wife can be replaced, but the loss of character spells ruin.

MALAY PROVERB

Where there is marriage without love, there will be love without marriage.

BENJAMIN FRANKLIN (1706–1790)

I don't think I'll get married again. I'll just find a woman I don't like and give her a house.

LEWIS GRIZZARD (1947–1994)

I'd marry again if I found a man who had 15 million and would sign over half of it to me before the marriage and guarantee he'd be dead within a year.

BETTE DAVIS (1908–1989)

I don't believe man is woman's natural enemy. Perhaps his lawyer is.

SHANA ALEXANDER (B. 1925)

I was married by a judge. I should have asked for a jury.

GROUCHO MARX (1890–1977)

Never go to bed mad. Stay up and fight.

PHYLLIS DILLER (B. 1917)

If it weren't for marriage, men and women would have to fight with total strangers.

ANONYMOUS

Whilst you are proclaiming peace and good will to men, you insist upon retaining an absolute power over wives. . . . Do not put such unlimited power into the hands of the husbands. Remember, all men would be tyrants if they could.

ABIGAIL ADAMS IN A LETTER TO JOHN ADAMS
(31 MARCH 1776).

———•••———

The comfortable estate of widowhood is the only hope that keeps up a wife's spirits.

JOHN GAY
THE BEGGAR'S OPERA (1728)

———•••———

Marriage is the wastepaper basket of the emotions.

SIDNEY WEBB (1859–1947)

Before marriage, a man will lie awake all night thinking about something you said; after marriage, he'll fall asleep before you finish saying it.

HELEN ROWLAND (1875–1950)

Accident counts for much in companionship as in marriage.

HENRY BROOK ADAMS
THE EDUCATION OF HENRY ADAMS (1918)

Love comes from blindness, friendship from knowledge.

COMTE DE BUSSY-RABUTIN
HISTOIRE AMOUREUSE DES GAULES (1665)

Wives are young men's mistresses, companions for middle age, and old men's nurses.

FRANCIS BACON
"OF MARRIAGE AND SINGLE LIFE" (1601)

By all means marry. If you get a good wife you will become happy, and if you get a bad one you will become a philosopher.

SOCRATES (469–399 B.C.)

She was a worthy woman al hir lyve:
Housbondes at chirche dore she hadde fyve.

GEOFFREY CHAUCER
THE CANTERBURY TALES (C. 1387)

I say to the unmarried . . . that it is good for them if they remain [celibate] even as I. But if they do not have self-control, let them marry, for it is better to marry than to burn.

PAUL TO THE CORINTHIANS I, 7:8–9

There are good marriages, but no delightful ones.

LA ROCHEFOUCAULD (1613–1680)

Marriage is a desperate thing.

JOHN SELDEN
TABLE TALK (1689)

At first a woman doesn't want anything but a husband, but just as soon as she gets one, she wants everything in the world.

EDGAR WATSON HOWE
COUNTRY TOWN SAYINGS (1911)

A lifetime of happiness! No man could bear it; it would be hell on earth.

GEORGE BERNARD SHAW
MAN AND SUPERMAN (1905)

———

Marriage is a great institution, but who wants to live in an institution?

GROUCHO MARX (1890–1977)

———

Marriage is popular because it combines the maximum of temptation with the maximum of opportunity.

GEORGE BERNARD SHAW (1856–1950)

My definition of marriage . . . it resembles a pair of shears, so joined that they cannot be separated; often moving in opposite directions, yet always punishing anyone who comes between them.

SYDNEY SMITH, QUOTED IN *A MEMOIR OF REVEREND SYDNEY SMITH BY HIS DAUGHTER, LADY HOLLAND* (1855).

If variety is the spice of life, marriage is the big can of leftover Spam.

JOHNNY CARSON (B. 1925)

A good marriage is like a casserole, only those responsible for it really know what goes in it.

ANONYMOUS

I've been married so long I'm on my third bottle of Tabasco sauce.

SUSAN VASS (N.D.)

My brother Toby, quoth she, is going to be married to Mrs. Wadman.
Then he will never, quoth my father, lie diagonally in his own bed again as long as he lives.

LAURENCE STERNE
TRISTRAM SHANDY (1759–1767)

Keep your eyes wide open before marriage, and half shut afterwards.

BENJAMIN FRANKLIN (1706–1790)

Marriage is like life in this—that it is a field of battle, and not a bed of roses.

ROBERT LOUIS STEVENSON
VIRGINIBUS PUERISQUE (1881)

Marriage is the only war in which you sleep with the enemy.

ANONYMOUS

Marriage should always combat the monster that devours everything: habit.

HONORÉ DE BALZAC
PHYSIOLOGIE DU MARIAGE (1829)

Marriage from love, like vinegar from wine—A sad, sour, sober beverage—by time.

LORD BYRON
DON JUAN (1821)

So that is marriage, Lily thought, a man and a woman looking at a girl throwing a ball.

VIRGINIA WOOLF
TO THE LIGHTHOUSE (1927)

He was reputed one of the wise men that made answer to the question when a man should marry? "A young man not yet, an elder man not at all."

FRANCIS BACON
"OF MARRIAGE AND SINGLE LIFE" (1601)

Advice to persons about to marry—"Don't."

PUNCH MAGAZINE

5

The Battle of the Sexes

> *The silliest woman can manage a clever man, but it takes a very clever woman to manage a fool.*
>
> —RUDYARD KIPLING

Throughout history, men and women have warred nearly as much as they've wooed. And why not?—the heightened emotions of an argument often lead to an outpouring of passion. It's the yin-yang of sexual attraction, the way we almost resent the person we want most, the one who holds the greatest power over us.

A top spot in the spar wars goes to Beatrice and Benedick from Shakespeare's *Much Ado About Nothing*. Rarely has a couple argued so skillfully—or so thrillingly. We await their capitulation with bated breath and are pleased to discover that, since they are equally helpless in the face of love, we find them equals still at the end of the play.

The Taming of the Shrew is another stirring example of love as a battlefield. (Do we get the impression that Shakespeare himself was no stranger to uppity women?) Petruchio believes he has mastered

Kate at the end, but the audience knows it is she who has ultimately tamed her swaggering suitor.

From Eleanor of Aquitaine and Henry II to Eliza Doolittle and Henry Higgins to Marge and Homer Simpson, couples have always practiced one-upmanship on each other. TV sitcoms from the 1950s onward are full of wise, all-knowing wives and dunderheaded husbands who try to outwit them. Perhaps this is womankind's revenge—having gotten short shrift in the ruling-the-world department, she's determined to rule over her spouse. Whatever the reason, sparks fly when male ego meets female superego.

Still, there are benefits to a good quarrel between lovers—they get to test the limits of affection, exorcise anger before it starts to fester, gain an understanding of their partner and, most important of all, learn the art of forgiveness. And then, of course there's that great make-up sex . . .

Love is like the measles; we all have to go through it.

JEROME K. JEROME
THE IDLE THOUGHTS OF AN IDLE FELLOW (1886)

Love's like the measles—all the worse when it comes late in life.

DOUGLAS JERROLD
"A PHILANTHROPIST" (1859)

Love, in the form in which it exists in society, is nothing but the exchange of two fantasies and the superficial contact of two bodies.

SÉBASTIEN-ROCH-NICOLAS CHAMFORT (1741–1794)

We owe to the Middle Ages the two worst inventions of humanity—romantic love and gunpowder.

ANDRÉ MAUROIS (1885–1967)

In expressing love, we belong among the undeveloped countries.

SAUL BELLOW (B. 1915)

Romance at short notice was her specialty.

SAKI
BEASTS AND SUPER-BEASTS (1914)

Love is the emotion that a woman feels always for a poodle dog and sometimes for a man.

GEORGE JEAN NATHAN
THE THEATER, THE DRAMA AND THE GIRLS (1921)

Women and cats will do as they please. Men and dogs had better get used to it.

ROBERT HEINLEIN
TIME ENOUGH FOR LOVE (1973)

A lover tries to stand in well with the pet dog of the house.

MOLIÈRE (1622–1673)

Lovely female shapes are terrible complicators of the difficulties and dangers of this earthly life, especially to their owners.

GEORGE DU MAURIER
TRILBY (1894)

The reason lovers never tire of each other is this: they're always talking about themselves.

LA ROCHEFOUCAULD
MAXIMS (1665)

Love is an emotion experienced by the many and enjoyed by the few.

GEORGE JEAN NATHAN (1882–1958)

When Jamie Lee Curtis wants to seduce an uptight British barrister, she . . . tells him he is irresistible. This illustrates a universal law of human nature, that every man, no matter how resistible, believes that when a woman in a low-cut dress tells him such things she must certainly be saying the truth.

ROGER EBERT, REVIEWING *A FISH CALLED WANDA* (1988).

If love is the answer, could you please rephrase the question?

LILY TOMLIN (B. 1939)

Love is the answer, but while you're waiting for the answer, sex raises some pretty good questions.

WOODY ALLEN (B. 1935)

While it's true that love itself is not a solution, it offers the possibility of many solutions.

NANCY BUTLER
PROSPERO'S DAUGHTER (2003)

Nothing spoils a romance so much as a sense of humor in the woman—or the want of it in a man.

OSCAR WILDE
A WOMAN OF NO IMPORTANCE (1893)

Man forgives woman anything save the wit to outwit him.

MINNA ANTRIM (1861–1950)

Women upset everything. When you let them into your life, you find that the woman is driving at one thing and you're driving at another.

GEORGE BERNARD SHAW
PYGMALION (1913)

Women have served all these centuries as looking-glasses providing the magic and delicious power of reflecting the figure of a man as twice its natural size.

VIRGINIA WOOLF
A ROOM OF ONE'S OWN (1929)

I admit it is more fun to punt than to be punted, and that a desire to have all the fun is nine-tenths of the law of chivalry.

DOROTHY L. SAYERS
GAUDY NIGHT (1935)

I'm not denyin' the women are foolish: God Almighty made 'em to match the men.

GEORGE ELIOT (1819–1880)

———

Women are never disarmed by compliments; men always are.

OSCAR WILDE
AN IDEAL HUSBAND (C. 1895)

———

The only thing worse than a man you can't control is a man you can.

MARGO KAUFMAN (1953–2000)

To win a woman in the first place you must please her, then undress her, and then somehow get her clothes back on her. Finally, so that she will let you leave her, you've got to antagonize her.

JEAN GIRAUDOUX
AMPHITRYON (1929)

There were endless variations on the same theme. Men who took one look at their new child and went, men who took one look at their new colleague and went, men who went for the hell of it.

NICK HORNBY
ABOUT A BOY (1998)

Women want mediocre men, and men are working hard to become as mediocre as possible.

MARGARET MEAD (1901–1978)

A woman has got to love a bad man once or twice in her life, to be thankful for a good one.

MARJORIE KINNAN RAWLINGS
THE YEARLING (1938)

Never judge someone by who he's in love with; judge him by his friends. People fall in love with the most appalling people. Take a cool, appraising glance at his pals.

CYNTHIA HEIMEL (B. 1947)

Women like silent men. They think they're listening.

MARCEL ACHARD (1899–1974)

The first duty of love is to listen.

PAUL TILLICH (1886–1965)

Laugh and the world laughs with you. Snore and you sleep alone.

ANTHONY BURGESS (1917–1993)

A woman never sees what we do for her, only what we don't do.

GEORGES COURTELINE
LA PAIX CHEZ SOI (1903)

All women become like their mothers. That is their tragedy. No man does. That is his.

OSCAR WILDE (1854–1900)

The great question . . . which I have not been able to answer, despite my thirty years of research into the feminine soul, is "What does a woman want?"

SIGMUND FREUD (1856–1939)

Love is the delightful interval between meeting a beautiful girl and discovering she looks like a haddock.

JOHN BARRYMORE (1882–1942)

Man is a natural polygamist. He always has one woman leading him by the nose and another hanging on to his coattails.

HENRY LOUIS MENCKEN (1880–1956)

Imagine that men are from Mars and women are from Venus.

JOHN GRAY, PH.D.
MEN ARE FROM MARS, WOMEN ARE FROM VENUS (1992)

The boys and girls live in separate worlds. The boys in their universe and we in ours.

SANDRA CISNEROS
THE HOUSE ON MANGO STREET (1984)

Sometimes I wonder if men and women really suit each other. Maybe they should live next door and just visit now and then.

KATHARINE HEPBURN (B. 1907)

Ah, if we could find a little bungalow. Of course, I know we could find one, but the people might not move out.

Groucho Marx (1890–1977)

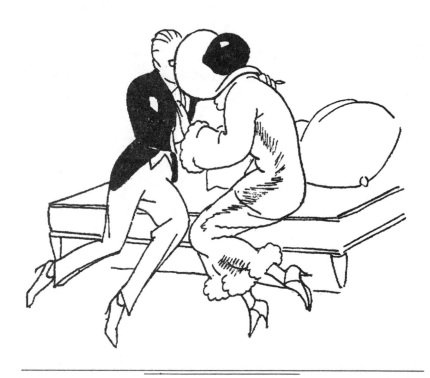

I love Mickey Mouse more than any woman I have ever known.

WALT DISNEY (1901–1966)

Love, love, love—all the wretched cant of it, masking egotism, lust, masochism, fantasy under a mythology of sentimental postures, a welter of self-induced miseries and joys, blinding and masking the essential personalities in the frozen gestures of courtship, in the kissing and the dating and the desire, the compliments and the quarrels which vivify its barrenness.

GERMAINE GREER
THE FEMALE EUNUCH (1970)

Love commingled with hate is more powerful than love. Or hate.

JOYCE CAROL OATES (B. 1938)

Falling in love is not an extension of one's limits or boundaries; it is a partial and temporary collapse of them.

M. SCOTT PECK
THE ROAD LESS TRAVELED (1978)

When Nature has made us ripe for Love it seldom occurs that the Fates are behindhand in furnishing a Temple for the flame.

GEORGE MEREDITH
THE ORDEAL OF RICHARD FEVEREL (1859)

We had a lot in common. I loved him and he loved him.

SHELLEY WINTERS (B. 1922)

Tis woman that seduces all mankind;
By her we first were taught the wheedling arts.

> JOHN GAY
> *THE BEGGAR'S OPERA* (1728)

If there hadn't been women we'd still be squatting in a
cave eating raw meat, because we made civilization in
order to impress our girlfriends.

> ORSON WELLES (1915–1985)

Women are most fascinating creatures between the ages
of thirty-five and forty, after they have won a few races
and know how to pace themselves. Since few women
ever pass forty, maximum fascination can continue
indefinitely.

> CHRISTIAN DIOR
> *COLLIERS* (10 JUNE 1955)

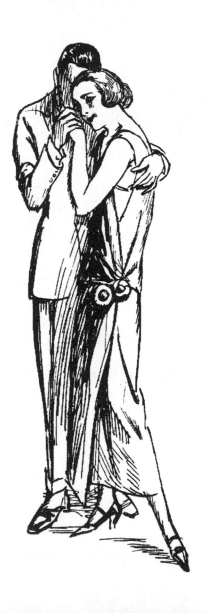

Why is it that every man I meet used up all his "nice" years on someone else, and only finds me when he is cranky and inflexible?

CATHY GUISEWITE (B. 1950)

A mother takes twenty years to make a man of her boy, and another woman makes a fool of him in twenty minutes.

ROBERT FROST (1874–1963)

Real love is a permanently self-enlarging experience. Falling in love is not.

M. SCOTT PECK
THE ROAD LESS TRAVELED (1978)

In literature as in love, we are astonished at what is chosen by others.

ANDRÉ MAUROIS (1885–1967)

There are three things men can do with women: love them, suffer for them, or turn them into literature.

STEPHEN STILLS (B. 1945)

When you're in love, you put up with things that, when you're out of love, you cite.

MISS MANNERS (B. 1938)

She was hardly more affable than a cameo.

SIR MAX BEERBOHM
ZULEIKA DOBSON (1911)

My friends have always given me that supreme proof of devotion, a spontaneous aversion for the man I loved.

COLETTE (1873–1954)

Mr. Right's coming, but he's in Africa, and he's walking!

OPRAH WINFREY (B. 1954)

Love and sex can go together and sex and unlove can go together and love and unsex can go together. But personal love and personal sex is bad.

ANDY WARHOL
FROM *A TO B AND BACK AGAIN* (1975)

In my sex fantasy, nobody ever loves me for my mind.

NORA EPHRON (B. 1941)

A god could hardly love and be wise.

> PUBLILIUS SYRUS
> *MAXIM* (C. 42 B.C.)

The four magic words to support a man are "It's not your fault."

> JOHN GRAY, PH.D.
> *MEN ARE FROM MARS, WOMEN ARE FROM VENUS* (1992)

If you go to see the woman, do not forget the whip.

> FRIEDRICH NIETZSCHE (1844–1900)

Love is like any other luxury. You have no right to it unless you can afford it.

> ANTHONY TROLLOPE
> *THE WAY WE LIVE NOW* (1875)

If I were a girl, I'd despair. The supply of good women far exceeds that of the men who deserve them.

ROBERT GRAVES (1895–1985)

There certainly are not so many men of large fortune in the world, as there are pretty women to deserve them.

JANE AUSTEN
MANSFIELD PARK (1814)

He promised me earrings, but he only pierced my ears.

ARABIAN SAYING

"Goodness, what beautiful diamonds."
"Goodness had nothing to do with it, dearie."
>   MAE WEST (1893–1980)

Kissing your hand may make you feel very very good but a diamond and sapphire bracelet lasts forever.
>   ANITA LOOS
>   *GENTLEMEN PREFER BLONDES* (1925)

It is possible that blondes also prefer gentlemen.
>   MAMIE VAN DOREN (B. 1933)

Gentlemen prefer bonds.
>   ANDREW MELLON (1855–1937)

Blonde or brunette, this rhyme applies,
Happy is he who knows them not.

FRANÇOIS VILLON (C. 1430–C. 1465)

Men are like a deck of cards. You'll find the occasional
king, but most are jacks.

LAURA SWENSON (N.D.)

What cannot a neat knave with a smooth tale
Make a woman believe?

JOHN WEBSTER
THE DUCHESS OF MALFI (1614)

Mad, bad, and dangerous to know.

LADY CAROLINE LAMB, WRITING IN HER JOURNAL ENTRY ABOUT
LORD BYRON.

O heaven, were man
But constant, he were perfect.

WILLIAM SHAKESPEARE
THE TWO GENTLEMEN OF VERONA (1594)

For the female of the species is more deadly than the male.

RUDYARD KIPLING
"THE FEMALE OF THE SPECIES" (1911)

Zuleika, on a desert island, would have spent most of her time in looking for a man's foot-print.

SIR MAX BEERBOHM
ZULEIKA DOBSON (1911)

... the most unnatural of the sexual perversions.

ALDOUS HUXLEY, WRITING ON CHASTITY.
EYELESS IN GAZA (1936)

Give me chastity and continency—but not yet.

ST. AUGUSTINE
CONFESSIONS (397–401)

Cherchons la femme.
Let us look for the woman.

ALEXANDRE DUMAS, PÈRE
LES MOHICANS DE PARIS (1854–1859)

A woman is only a woman, but a good cigar is a Smoke.
RUDYARD KIPLING (1865–1936)

Here's to woman! Would that we could fall into her arms without falling into her hands.
AMBROSE BIERCE, QUOTED IN *BITTER BIERCE* (1929).

A woman needs a man like a fish needs a bicycle.
GLORIA STEINEM (B. 1934)

6

Love on the Rocks

O! Swear not by the moon, the inconstant moon,
That monthly changes in her circled orb,
Lest that thy love prove likewise variable.
—WILLIAM SHAKESPEARE

There are no guarantees in love. The strongest, fiercest affection means little if it is not returned in kind. Even when passions are evenly matched, so much of the outside world intrudes on the lovers' intimate sphere—the demands of home and children, career stress, financial woes, and that old chestnut, the in-laws. Often couples are drawn apart by circumstance—literature is full of faithful Evangelines and Penelopes—or by the weight of society's censure, as in *Anna Karenina*. Jealousy, infidelity, the lure of drink and gambling, all lie in wait to trip up love and make it falter. Sometimes it is merely callow youth that is at fault—many an immature lover has regretted that the perfect partner "who got away" did not appear slightly later in life. Timing, as we know, is everything.

Fortunately, when love abandons us, the inspiration to create often fills the void. The number of poems, songs, novels, plays, and essays devoted to lost love is staggering. You could sink a battleship with the collected verse of college students suffering the break-up blues. And has anyone in country music actually had a lover who stuck around past the closing credits of *Hee-Haw?*

Even though breaking up is hard to do, a failed romance offers us some insight on how to handle things better the next time. And there's always a next time . . . the human animal, in true hunter-gatherer fashion, is always moving on, looking for new sport. And even if we are a bit heartsore, if not downright heartbroken, we keep the spark of hope alive. Because for all we know, new love, maybe better love, is right around the next corner.

I am a lover and have not found my thing to love.

SHERWOOD ANDERSON
WINESBURG, OHIO (1919)

Love lives in sealed bottles of regret.

SEÁN O'FAOLÁIN
"THE JUNGLE OF LOVE," *SATURDAY EVENING POST*
(AUGUST 1966)

I don't love you, Sabidius, and I can't tell you why; all I can tell you is this, that I don't love you.

MARTIAL
EPIGRAMMATA (C. A.D. 64)

A man who has never made a woman angry is a failure in life.

CHRISTOPHER MORLEY (1890–1957)

Love means not ever having to say you're sorry.
ERICH SEGAL
LOVE STORY (1970)

———

Alimony is always having to say you're sorry.
PHILIP J. SIMBORG (N.D.)

———

Love is a hole in the heart.
BEN HECHT (1894–1964)

———

Love has its reasons that reason knows nothing of.
BLAISE PASCAL
PENSÉES (1660)

Trouble is a part of your life, and if you don't share it, you don't give the person that loves you enough chance to love you enough.

> DINAH SHORE (1917–1994)

———•••———

One's head is invariably the dupe of one's heart.

> LA ROCHEFOUCAULD
> *REFLECTIONS* (1665)

———•••———

It's very hard to get your heart and head together in life. In my case, they're not even friendly.

> WOODY ALLEN
> *HUSBANDS AND WIVES* (1992)

Love is an attempt to change a piece of a dream world into reality.

THEODOR REIK, RECALLED ON HIS DEATH (31 DECEMBER 1969).

———

Hideous, wasted two days glaring psychopathically at the phone, and eating things. Why hasn't he wrung?

HELEN FIELDING
BRIDGET JONES'S DIARY (1996)

———

It seems that it is madder never to abandon one's self than often to be infatuated; better to be wounded, a captive and a slave, than always to walk in armor.

MARGARET FULLER
SUMMER ON THE LAKES (1844)

The big question in life is the unhappiness one has caused; . . . the most ingenious rationalizations will not help the man who has broken the heart he loved.

BENJAMIN CONSTANT
ADOLPHE (1816)

Love must precede hatred, and nothing is hated save through being contrary to a suitable thing which is loved. And hence it is that every hatred is caused by love.

ST. THOMAS AQUINAS
SUMMA THEOLOGICA (1273)

Love is whatever you can still betray. . . . Betrayal can only happen if you love.

JOHN LE CARRÉ
A PERFECT SPY (1986)

Hell, Madame, is to love no longer.

GEORGE BERNANOS
THE DIARY OF A COUNTRY PRIEST (1936)

———

Love gratified is love satisfied, and love satisfied is indifference begun.

SAMUEL RICHARDSON
CLARISSA (1747)

———

Of all the objects of hatred, a woman once loved is the most hateful.

SIR MAX BEERBOHM
ZULEIKA DOBSON (1911)

The heaviest object in the world is the body of the woman you have ceased to love.

MARQUIS DE LUC DE CLAPIERS VAUVENARGUES (1715–1747)

How much the heart may bear, and yet not break!

ELIZABETH AKERS ALLEN (1832–1911)

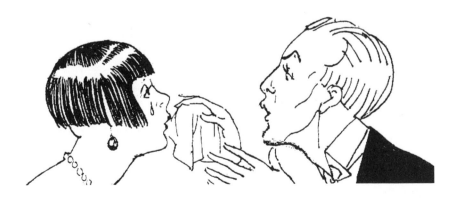

Love sickness needs a love cure.

CHINESE PROVERB

Full many a flower is born to blush unseen,
And waste its sweetness on the desert air.

THOMAS GRAY
"ELEGY IN A COUNTRY CHURCHYARD" (1750)

Mortal love is but the licking of honey from thorns.

ANONYMOUS WOMAN AT THE COURT OF ELEANOR OF AQUITAINE

Fickle and changeable always is a woman.

> VIRGIL
> *AENEID* (19 B.C.)

———

The fickleness of the woman I love is only equaled by the infernal constancy of the women who love me.

> GEORGE BERNARD SHAW (1856–1950)

———

I have been faithful to thee, Cynara! in my fashion.

> ERNEST DOWSON (1867–1900)

I'm an excellent housekeeper. Every time I get a divorce,
I keep the house.

ZSA ZSA GABOR (B. 1919)

Time wounds all heels.

JANE ACE (1905–1974)

And the best and the worst of this is
That neither is most to blame
If you have forgotten my kisses
And I have forgotten your name.

ALGERNON CHARLES SWINBURNE (1837–1909)

Those who are faithful know only the trivial side of love;
it is the faithless who know love's tragedies.

OSCAR WILDE
THE PICTURE OF DORIAN GRAY (1890)

Sure men were born to lie, and women to believe them.

JOHN GAY
THE BEGGAR'S OPERA (1728)

Eighty percent of married men cheat in America. The rest
cheat in Europe.

JACKIE MASON (B. 1934)

Jealousy is not a barometer by which depth of love can be read. It merely records the degree of the lover's insecurity.

MARGARET MEAD (1901–1978)

The quarrels of lovers are the renewal of love.

TERENCE
ANDRIA (C. 166 B.C.)

If you judge people, you have no time to love them.

MOTHER TERESA (1910–1997)

Men are always doomed to be duped, not so much by the arts of the [female] sex as by their own imaginations. They are always wooing goddesses and marrying mere mortals.

WASHINGTON IRVING
BRACEBRIDGE HALL (1822)

To be in love is merely to be in a state of perceptual anaesthesia—to mistake an ordinary young man for a Greek god or an ordinary young woman for a goddess.

H. L. MENCKEN
PREJUDICES (1919–1927)

If only one could tell true love from false love as one can tell mushrooms from toadstools.

KATHERINE MANSFIELD (1888–1923)

In how many lives does Love really play a dominant part? The average taxpayer is no more capable of a "grand passion" than of a grand opera.

ISRAEL ZANGWILL (1864–1926)

———

[The] common men-in-the-street and women-in-the-street . . . have as great a hate and contempt for sex as the greyest Puritan. . . . They insist that a film heroine shall be neuter . . . that real sex feelings shall only be shown by the villain or villainess . . .

D. H. LAWRENCE
"PORNOGRAPHY AND OBSCENITY," *THIS QUARTER* (1929)

———

It is never any good dwelling on goodbyes. It is not the being together that it prolongs, it is the parting.

ELIZABETH ASQUITH BIBESCO
THE FIR AND THE PALM (1924)

If you love somebody, let them go. If they return, they were always yours. If they don't, they never were.

ANONYMOUS

Love is like playing checkers. You have to know which man to move.

JACKIE "MOMS" MABLEY (1894–1975)

Had we never lov'd sae kindly,
Had we never lov'd sae blindly,
Never met—or never parted,
We had ne'er been broken-hearted.

ROBERT BURNS (1759–1796)

The way to love anything is to realize that it might be lost.

G. K. CHESTERTON (1874–1936)

⸺•⸺

In a separation it is the one who is not really in love who says the more tender things.

MARCEL PROUST
REMEMBRANCE OF THINGS PAST (1922–1931)

⸺•⸺

Let's be independent as hell. Let's each fly in different directions and wonder why for the rest of our lives.

JAMES HILTON
RANDOM HARVEST (1941)

'Tis better to have loved and lost, than never to have loved at all.

SAMUEL BUTLER
THE WAY OF ALL FLESH (1903)

Say what you will, 'tis better to be left than never to have been loved.

WILLIAM CONGREVE
THE WAY OF THE WORLD (1700)

Since there's no help, come, let us kiss and part.

MICHAEL DRAYTON (1563–1631)

O sad kissed mouth, how sorrowful it is!

ALGERNON CHARLES SWINBURNE (1837–1909)

A man never knows how to say goodbye; a woman never knows when to say it.

HELEN ROWLAND
REFLECTIONS OF A BACHELOR GIRL (1903)

Take me or leave me, or, as is the usual order of things, both.

DOROTHY PARKER
"A GOOD NOVEL, AND A GREAT STORY,"
(*THE NEW YORKER*, 1928)

We are never so defenseless against suffering as when we love, never so helplessly unhappy as when we have lost our love object or its love.

SIGMUND FREUD
CIVILIZATION AND ITS DISCONTENTS (1930)

The great tragedy of life is not that men perish, but that they cease to love.

W. SOMERSET MAUGHAM
THE SUMMING UP (1938)

The heart that can no longer
Love passionately, must with fury hate.

JEAN RACINE
ANDROMACHE (1667)

Yet each man kills the thing he loves,
By each let this be heard. . . .
The coward does it with a kiss,
The brave man with a sword.

OSCAR WILDE
"THE BALLAD OF READING GAOL" (1898)

7

Endless Love

None shall part us from each other,
One in life and death are we:
All in all to one another—
I to thee and thou to me!
—Sir William S. Gilbert

When love endures in spite of the passage of time, it strikes a lasting chord in our collective imaginations. We marvel at the couples, both real and fictional, who have not let the light of mutual devotion fade. Either the power of their love exalts us, or their tragedy brings us to tears—and frequently it does both. Antony and Cleopatra, Caesar and Cleopatra, Eloise and Abelard, Tristan and Isolde, Robin and Marian, Arthur and Guinevere, Lancelot and Guinevere (was she taking lessons from Cleo?), Dante and Beatrice, Romeo and Juliet, Ivanhoe and Rowena, Horatio Nelson and Emma Hamilton, Napoleon and Josephine, Scarlet and Rhett, Victoria and Albert, Bogart and Bacall . . . the list goes on and on.

Often their stories came to us from oral tradition and ballads or, in more recent times, in the form of letters. Great loves lend themselves to great literature, and few authors are proof against the drama and scope they afford.

Yet, what is it that gives these romances a place in our hearts? Perhaps it is knowing that the couples loved in spite of great odds, and that even if they were separated, their passion did not die. They are the exemplars of endless love; the sort we want to believe exists, if only between the covers of a book. When steadfast love does occur in real life (or in the mythos of real life) we are transported.

True love isn't the kind that endures through long years of absence, but the kind that endures through long years of propinquity.

HELEN ROWLAND
A GUIDE TO MEN (1922)

Immature love says: "I love you because I need you." Mature love says: "I need you because I love you."

ERICH FROMM
THE ART OF LOVING (1956)

When I died, I wanted Sallie to say when she kissed me for the last time, "I chose the right man."

PAT CONROY
THE PRINCE OF TIDES (1986)

The love we have in our youth is superficial compared to the love that an old man has for his old wife.

> WILL DURANT, ON HIS 90TH BIRTHDAY, *NEW YORK TIMES* (NOVEMBER 1975).

Age does not protect you from love but love to some extent protects you from age.

> JEANNE MOREAU (B. 1928)

If grass can grow through cement, love can find you at every time in your life.

> CHER (B. 1946)

One is never too old for romance.

> INGRID BERGMAN
> *SUNDAY MIRROR* (5 MAY 1974)

The highest level of sexual excitement is in a monogamous relationship.

WARREN BEATTY
OBSERVER (27 OCTOBER 1991)

Escape me?
Never—
Beloved!

> ROBERT BROWNING
> "LIFE IN A LOVE" (1855)

How do I love thee? Let me count the ways.

> ELIZABETH BARRETT BROWNING
> SONNETS FROM THE PORTUGUESE (1850)

Was this the face that launch'd a thousand ships,
And burnt the topless towers of Ilium?
Sweet Helen, make me immortal with a kiss.

> CHRISTOPHER MARLOWE
> DR. FAUSTUS (C. 1588)

If the nose of Cleopatra had been shorter, the whole face of the earth would have been changed.

> BLAISE PASCAL
> *PENSÉES* (1660)

———

She shall be buried by her Antony:
No grave upon the earth shall clip in it
A pair so famous.

> WILLIAM SHAKESPEARE
> *ANTONY AND CLEOPATRA* (C. 1606)

———

We fluctuate long between love and hatred before we can arrive at tranquility.

> HELOISE, IN HER FIRST LETTER TO ABELARD (C. 1122).

Let not poor Nelly starve.

KING CHARLES II (1630–1685)

Pray, good people, be civil. I am the Protestant whore.

NELL GWYN (1650–1687)

My only love sprung from my only hate!

JULIET TO ROMEO, IN WILLIAM SHAKESPEARE,
ROMEO AND JULIET (1597).

Call me but love, and I'll be new baptized;
Henceforth I never will be Romeo.

ROMEO TO JULIET, IN WILLIAM SHAKESPEARE,
ROMEO AND JULIET (1597).

It was with some emotion . . . that I beheld Albert—who is beautiful.

> QUEEN VICTORIA ON HER FIRST MEETING WITH THE PRINCE CONSORT (C. 1838).

P. S. It's all gossip about the prince. I'm not in the habit of taking my girlfriend's beaux.

> WALLIS WARFIELD SIMPSON, WHO DID EXACTLY THAT (1934).

I love you more than my own skin.

> FRIDA KAHLO, IN A LETTER TO HUSBAND, DIEGO RIVERA (1935).

There's a great woman behind every idiot.

JOHN LENNON, SPEAKING OF WIFE, YOKO ONO.

———

Please fence me in baby. The world's too big out here and I don't like it without you.

HUMPHREY BOGART, IN A TELEGRAM TO LAUREN BACALL.

———

I don't sit around thinking that I'd like to have another husband; only another man would make me think that way.

LAUREN BACALL (B. 1924)

So you wound up with Apollo
If he's sometimes hard to swallow
Use this.

PAUL NEWMAN, INSCRIPTION ON SHERRY CUP FOR WIFE,
JOANNE WOODWARD.
NEW YORK TIMES (28 SEPTEMBER 1986).

I've been asked to say a couple of words about my husband, Fang. How about "short" and "cheap"?

PHYLLIS DILLER (B. 1917)

Caitlin. Just to write down your name like that. Caitlin. I don't have to say My Dear. My Darling.

DYLAN THOMAS (1914–1953)

The Duke returned from the wars today and did pleasure me in his top-boots.

SARAH, 1ST DUCHESS OF MARLBOROUGH (1660–1744)

Reader, I married him.

CHARLOTTE BRONTË
JANE EYRE (1846)

I am Heathcliff—he's always, always in my mind—not as a pleasure, any more than I am a pleasure to myself—but as my own being.

EMILY BRONTË
WUTHERING HEIGHTS (1847)

Whither thou goest, I will go . . . thy people shall be my people and thy God, my God.

THE BOOK OF RUTH 1:16

———•••———

I love you Scarlett, because we are so much alike, renegades, both of us, dear, and selfish rascals. Neither of us cares a rap if the whole world goes to pot, so long as we are safe and comfortable.

MARGARET MITCHELL
GONE WITH THE WIND (1936)

———•••———

It was Rhett . . . because he, like her, saw truth as truth, unobstructed by impractical notions of honor, sacrifice, or high belief in human nature.

MARGARET MITCHELL
GONE WITH THE WIND (1936)

You, my own Emma, are my first and last thoughts, and to the last moment of my breath they will be occupied in leaving you independent of the World.

HORATIO NELSON TO EMMA HAMILTON (1805).

My soul is in your body.

NAPOLEON BONAPARTE TO JOSEPHINE (1796).

It was a very spasmodic courtship, conducted mainly at long distance with a great clanking of coins in dozens of phone booths.

JACQUELINE KENNEDY ONASSIS, ON HER ROMANCE WITH JOHN F. KENNEDY (QUOTED IN 1987).

I thought he was nuts or something.

PAT NIXON, ON HER FUTURE HUSBAND'S HABIT OF DRIVING HER OUT ON DATES WITH OTHER MEN.

I embrace my little cockroach and send her a million kisses.

ANTON CHEKHOV, TO HIS WIFE, ACTRESS OLGA KNIPPER (1904).

Dear Miss West . . . Am a widower with 10,000 acres in Arizona and seven cows so if you can milk I will be glad to have you give up that tinsel life of debauchery and sin and come out to God's country.
P.S. Can you bring a little sin and debauchery along?

JOHN STEINBECK, TO ELAINE SCOTT, FUTURE WIFE (1949).

I might run from her for a thousand years and she is still my baby child. . . . Our love is so furious that we burn each other out.

RICHARD BURTON ON ELIZABETH TAYLOR, RECALLED AT HIS DEATH (1984).

There was a reason he hadn't spoken and it had nothing to do with gray cells working. He hadn't spoken . . . because there was nothing for him to say. He didn't love her and that was that.

> BUTTERCUP'S THOUGHTS OF WESLEY, IN WILLIAM GOLDMAN, *THE PRINCESS BRIDE* (1973).

As you wish.

> WESLEY TO BUTTERCUP, IN WILLIAM GOLDMAN, THE PRINCESS BRIDE (1973).

To be able to say how much you love is to love but little.

> PETRARCH
> "TO LAURA IN DEATH" (C. 1300)

The fate of love is that it always seems too little or too much.

> ANONYMOUS

The love that lasts longest is the love that is never returned.

W. SOMERSET MAUGHAM, RECALLED ON HIS DEATH (DECEMBER 1965).

All the privilege I claim for my own sex . . . is that of loving longest, when existence or when hope is gone.

JANE AUSTEN
PERSUASION (1818)

Love is an act of endless forgiveness, a tender look which becomes a habit.

PETER USTINOV
CHRISTIAN SCIENCE MONITOR (DECEMBER 1958).

———

Love has meaning only insofar as it includes the idea of its continuance. Even what we rather glibly call a love affair, if it comes to an end, may continue as a memory that is pleasing in our lives. . . . But Lust dies at the next dawn.

HENRY FAIRLIE
"LUST," *THE SEVEN DEADLY SINS TODAY* (1978)

———

Many waters cannot quench love, neither can the floods drown it.

SONG OF SOLOMON 8:7

Love and memory last and will so endure till the game is called because of darkness.

> GENE FOWLER
> *SKYLINE* (1961)

———•••———

For how many people are there who have the memory of a whole long day and a whole long night, shining and sweet, to carry with them in their hearts until they die?

> DOROTHY PARKER
> "THE LOVELY LEAVE" (1920)

———•••———

Love vanquishes time. To lovers, a moment can be eternity, eternity can be the tick of a clock.

> MARY PARRISH
> "ALL THE LOVE IN THE WORLD" (*MCCALL'S* JUNE 1961)

Love me still, but know not why!

ANONYMOUS

———

It was a deep and desperate time-need, a clock ticking with his heart, and it urged him, against the whole logic of his life, to walk past her into the house now and say, "This is forever."

F. SCOTT FITZGERALD
THE LAST TYCOON (1941)

Who's Who

Ace, Goodman (1899–1982), American radio personality and partner of Jane.

Ace, Jane (1905–1974), American radio personality and partner of Goodman.

Achard, Marcel (1899–1974), French writer, actor, and director.

Ackerman, Diane (b. 1948), American poet, essayist, and naturalist.

Adams, Abigail (1744–1818), loyal wife of President John Adams.

Adams, Henry Brook (1838–1918), American writer and historian.

Ade, George (1866–1944), American anti-imperialist writer of satirical fables.

Alexander, Shana (b. 1925), American journalist and editor.

Allen, Elizabeth Akers (1832–1911), American poet and journalist.

Allen, Woody (b. 1935), American comic, director, author, and jazz musician.

Anderson, Sherwood (1876–1941), American playwright.

Andrews, Julie (b. 1935), brisk English stage and screen actress.

Anspacher, Louis Kaufman (1878–1947), American screenwriter and director.

Antrim, Minna (1861–1950), Irish writer.

Aquinas, St. Thomas (c. 1225–1274), Italian philosopher and theologian.

Aristophanes (448?–380 B.C.), Athenian dramatist.

Arnold, Matthew (1822–1888), English poet.

Ashley, Elizabeth (b. 1941), southern siren stage and screen actress.

Astor, Viscountess, Nancy Langhorne (1879–1964), first female member of the British Parliament.

Augustine, St., of Hippo (c. 350–430), early Christian theologian, one of the four Latin fathers.

Austen, Jane (1775–1817), British novelist and astute observer of the gentry class.

Bacall, Lauren (b. 1924), sultry film actress; "Baby" to Bogey.

Bacon, Francis (1561–1626), English philosopher, essayist, and statesman.

Balzac, Honoré de (1799–1850), racy French novelist.

Bankhead, Tallulah (1903–1968), whiskey-voiced American actress.

Barney, Natalie (1876–1972), American ex-patriot writer French salonist.

Barrie, J. M. (1860–1937), fanciful British writer.

Barry, Lynda (b. 1956), American cult-favorite writer, artist, and cartoonist.

Barrymore, John (1882–1942), flamboyant American actor.

Beatty, Warren (b. 1937), American actor.

Beerbohm, Sir Max (1872–1956), English essayist, caricaturist, and parodist.

Bellow, Saul (b. 1915), Canadian-born American novelist and Nobel Prize winner.

Bergman, Ingrid (1915–1982), Swedish-born actress specializing in strong, dignified women.

Berle, Milton (1908–2002), pioneer comic of early TV.

Bernanos, George (1888–1948), French essayist and novelist.

Bibesco, Elizabeth Asquith, Princess (1897–1945), British novelist and member of the famed Asquith family.

Bierce, Ambrose (1842–1914?), dark–humored American writer.

Binder, Mike (n.d.), American actor, director, writer, and producer.

Bisset, Jacqueline (b. 1944), glowing British actress.

Boethius (Anicius Manlius Severinus) (c. 480–525), Roman philosopher, poet, and politician.

Bogan, Louise (1897–1970), American poet.

Bogart, Humphrey (1899–1957), hardboiled American actor.

Bombeck, Erma (1927–1996), American author; the housewife's voice of reason.

Bonaparte, Napoleon (1769–1821), Corsican-born general and emperor of France.

Braisted, Harry, 19th-century American poet.

Brontë, Charlotte (1816–1855), English author of *Jane Eyre*.

Brontë, Emily (1818–1848), English author of *Wuthering Heights*.

Browning, Elizabeth Barrett (1806–1861), English poet, runaway bride of Robert Browning.

Browning, Robert (1812–1889), influential English poet.

Bulwer-Lytton, Edward Robert, 1st Earl of Lytton (1831–1891), much-parodied English poet, who gave us the seminal opening line, "It was a dark and stormy night . . ."

Burgess, Anthony (1917–1993), inventive and prolific British writer and linguistics expert.

Burns, Robert (1759–1796), beloved sentimental Scottish poet.

Burton, Richard (1925–1984), commanding Welsh stage and screen actor.

Bush, Barbara (b. 1925), First Lady, wife of George Bush.

Bussy–Rabutin, Roger, Comte de (1618–1693), French nobleman.

Butler, Samuel (1835–1902), English author.

Byron, George Gordon Noel Byron, 6th Baron (1788–1824), English romance poet and satirist.

Campbell, Mrs. Patrick (1865–1940), British actress and vivacious correspondent.

Campbell, Thomas (1777–1844), Scottish poet best known for his war poems.

Carroll, Jonathan (b. 1949), New York–born writer.

Carson, Johnny (b. 1925), American humorist and long-time host of TV's the *Tonight Show*.

Cartland, Barbara (1901–2000), syrupy English romance novelist.

Cary, Joyce (1888–1957), British novelist.

Cervantes, Miguel de (1547–1616), Spanish novelist, dramatist, and poet.

Chagall, Marc (1887–1985), Russian-born painter who lived in France.

Chamfort, Sébastien-Roch-Nicolas (1741–1794), French writer.

Chandler, Raymond (1888–1959), American author, creator of detective Philip Marlowe.

Charles II (1630–1685), Stuart monarch of the English Restoration.

Chase, Alexander (b. 1926), U.S. journalist, editor.

Chaucer, Geoffrey (c. 1340–1400), English poet and master story-teller.

Chekhov, Anton Pavlovich (1860–1904), Russian author, playwright.

Cher (Cherilyn LaPiere Sarkisian) (b. 1946), American entertainer and glamour icon.

Chesterton, G. K. (1874–1936), conservative English author.

Chevalier, Maurice (1888–1972), charming French actor and bon vivant.

Chopra, Deepak (b. 1947), Indian-born New-Age guru and bestselling author.

Christie, Dame Agatha (1890–1976), prolific British writer of mysteries.

Cisneros, Sandra (b. 1954), luminious novelist, short-story writer, essayist, and poet.

Colette (Sidonie-Gabrielle) (1873–1954), sparkling French author.

Congreve, William (1670–1729), British playwright.

Connolly, Cyril (1903–1974), English essayist.

Conroy, Pat (b. 1945), American novelist.

Constant, Benjamin (1767–1830), French-Swiss political writer and novelist.

Courteline, Georges (1858–1929), prolific French writer and satirist.

Crawford, Joan (1908–1977), no–nonsense American actress.

cummings, e e (1894–1962), eccentric American poet.

Davis, Bette (1908–1989), acerbic American actress.

Dickens, Charles (1812–1870), prodigiously productive English Victorian author.

Diderot, Denis (1713–1784), French encyclopedist.

Dietrich, Marlene (1901–1992), smoldering German-born film actress.

Diller, Phyllis (b. 1917), American comedienne and fashionista.

Dior, Christian (1905–1957), French couturier.

Disney, Walt (1901–1966), American animator and kingdom-maker.

Disraeli, Benjamin (1804–1881), British prime minister under Victoria and author.

Dix, Dorothea (1802–1887), American social reform pioneer.

Donne, John (1572–1631), British philosopher poet.

Dowson, Ernest (1867–1900), English lyric poet.

Drayton, Michael (1563–1631), English poet.

Dumas, Alexandre, *fils* (1824–1895), French novelist and dramatist.

Dumas, Alexandre, *père* (1802–1870), sweeping French novelist and dramatist.

Du Maurier, Daphne (1907–1989), English author of haunting novels, most notably *Rebecca*.

Du Maurier, George (1834–1896), British artist and novelist.

Durant, Will (1885–1981), American historian and essayist.

Duras, Marguerite (1914–1996), unconventional French novelist.

Durst, Will (b. 1954), American political humorist.

Ebert, Roger (b. 1942), film critic extraordinaire.

Ebner–Eschenbach, Marie von (1830–1916), Austrian writer.

Einstein, Albert (1879–1955), German-born American physicist noted for his theory of relativity and his endearing absent-mindedness.

Eliot, George (Mary Ann Evans) (1819–1880), British novelist infamous to schoolchildren everywhere for writing *Silas Marner*.

Ellis, Havelock (1859–1939), English psychologist and author.

Ephron, Nora (b. 1941), American novelist and screenwriter.

Evans, Nicholas (b. 1950), London-based, best-selling author.

Fairlie, Henry (1924–1990), British author.

Fielding, Helen (b. 1958), brash British novelist.

Fitzgerald, Francis Scott Key (1896–1940), American novelist and voice of the Lost Generation.

Flaubert, Gustave (1821–1880), French novelist.

Forbes, Malcolm (1919–1990), New Jersey–born publishing magnate, art collector, and author.

Fosdick, Harry Emerson (1878–1969), American clergyman, pastor of Riverside Church in New York, whose radio addresses were broadcast nationally.

Fowler, Gene (1890–1960), American journalist and biographer.

France, Anatole (Jacques Anatole Thibault) (1844–1924), French writer and satirist.

Franken, Rose (1895–1988), Texas-born playwright and director.

Franklin, Benjamin (1706–1790), American patriot and sage.

Freud, Sigmund (1856–1939), Austrian neurologist, founder of psychoanalysis.

Fromm, Erich (1900–1980), German-born American psychoanalyst.

Frost, Robert (1874–1963), American poet.

Fuller, (Sarah), Margaret (1810–1850), American critic and reformer.

Gabor, Zsa Zsa (b. 1919), Hungarian-born, much-married American actress.

Gace Brule (c. 1170–1212), nobleman poet from Champagne.

Galsworthy, John (1867–1933), Nobel Prize–winning English author and dramatist.

Gandhi, Mohandas (1869–1948), Hindu nationalist leader, pacifist, called Mahatma.

Garbo, Greta (1905–1990), elusive Swedish-born actress.

Garland, Judy (1922–1969), endearing singer and actress who took us "Over the Rainbow."

Garnett, Richard (1835–1906), English librarian and author.

Gay, John (1685–1732), English poet and dramatist.

Gibran, Kahlil (1883–1931), Syrian-born poet and novelist.

Gilbert, Sir William, S. (1836–1911), British lyricist.

Giovanni, Nikki (b. 1943), influential American poet, essayist, and lecturer.

Giraudoux, Jean (1882–1944), French writer.

Goldman, Emma (1869–1940), American political activist.

Goldman, William (b. 1931), American author and screenwriter.

Goncourt, the brothers (Edmont (1822–1896) and Jules (1830–1870), French writers.

Gorky, Maxim (1868–1936), Russian writer.

Graves, Robert (1895–1985), English poet, novelist, and critic.

Gray, John, Ph.D. (b. 1951), American relationship expert.

Gray, Thomas (1716–1771), English poet.

Greer, Germaine (b. 1939), Australian feminist writer.

Grizzard, Lewis (1947–1994), southern best-selling author and syndicated columnist.

Groening, Matt (b. 1954), acerbic American cartoonist turned animator and creator of *The Simpsons*.

Guisewite, Cathy (b. 1950), American cartoonist of *Cathy* fame.

Guitry, Sacha (1885–1957), dramatic French author, actor, and filmmaker.

Gwilym, Dafydd ap (1320–1370), greatest medieval Welsh poet.

Gwyn, Nell (1650–1687), famed Mistress of Charles II.

Hammurabi (c. 1792–1750 BC), King of Babylon known for his code of laws.

Hardwick, Elizabeth (b. 1916), Tennessee-born literary critic and novelist.

Hawthorne, Nathaniel (1804–1864), gloomy Salem-born novelist and short story writer.

Hayes, Helen (1900–1993), American screen actress and "First Lady of American Theater."

Hecht, Ben (1894–1964), prolific American playwright and screenwriter.

Heimel, Cynthia (b. 1947), contemporary author and columnist.

Heinlein, Robert (1907–1988), American science fiction writer.

Heller, Joseph (1923–1999), American novelist; voice of a disaffected age.

Heloise (c. 1101–1164), well-educated nun, writer, and lover of philosopher Peter Abelard.

Hemingway, Ernest (1899–1961), terse American novelist and short-story writer.

Henry, O. (William Henry Porter) (1862–1910), American short story writer known for ironic twist endings.

Hepburn, Katharine (b. 1907), coltish screen actress.

Herrick, Robert (1591–1674), greatest of the English Cavalier poets.

Hilton, James (1900–1954), English novelist and screenwriter.

Hite, Shere (b. 1943), American writer, feminist, and sex researcher.

Hoffman, Alice (b. 1952), New York–born novelist and short story writer.

Hoppe, Arthur (1925–2000), San Francisco journalist.

Hornby, Nick (b. 1957), best-selling British novelist, short story writer, and editor.

Howar, Barbara (b. 1934), American socialite and author.

Howe, Edgar Watson (1853–1937), pithy American editor and author.

Hubbard, Elbert (1856–1915), American author and publisher; advocate of rugged individualism.

Hugo, Victor (1802–1885), towering French novelist.

Hunt, Morton (b. 1920), American psychologist and author.

Hurston, Zora Neale (1891–1960), American author of short stories, novels, anthropological folklore, and an autobiography.

Huxley, Aldous (1894–1963), cynical but exuberant English author.

Ibsen, Henrik (1828–1906), Norwegian playwright given to symbolism.

Irving, Washington (1783–1859), American storyteller and diplomat, one of the first American men of letters to be recognized abroad.

James, Henry (1843–1916), American novelist and critic, master of the psychological novel.

Jerome, Jerome K. (1859–1927), English humorist.

Jerrold, Douglas (1803–1857), English humorist and playwright.

Jong, Erica (b. 1942), naughty New York–born novelist.

Kahlo, Frida (1907–1954), brilliant Mexican painter and wife of Diego Rivera.

Karr, Alphonse (1808–1890), French writer and editor of *Le Figaro*.

Kaufman, Margo (1953–2000), American columnist and humorist.

Kerr, Deborah (b. 1921), elegant British-born American actress.

Kerr, Jean (b. 1923), wry American dramatist and writer.

Kimball, Nell (1854–1934), American madam and writer.

King, Martin Luther, Jr. (1929–1968), American clergyman and civil rights leader.

Kipling, Rudyard (1865–1936), British colonial novelist and poet.

La Rochefoucauld, François, 7th duc de (1613–1680), French classical author.

Lamb, Lady Caroline (1785–1828), English writer, famous for her liaison with Byron.

Landers, Ann (Eppie Lederer) (1918–2002), widely syndicated American advice columnist.

Lanier, Sidney (1842–1881), Georgia-born poet and musician.

Lao-tzu (c. 570–490 B.C.), Chinese philosopher, accounted the founder of Taoism.

Lardner, Ring (1885–1933), American humorist and short story writer.

Lawrence, D. H. (1885–1930), controversial English author.

Le Carré, John (b. 1931), espionage novelist.

Leacock, Stephen (1869–1944), Canadian writer.

Leigh, Henry Sambrooke (1837–1883), British poet.

Lennon, John (1941–1980), British-born songwriter and performer, threw together a little foursome called The Beatles.

Lessing, Doris (b. 1919), energetic and well–traveled English author.

Lincoln, Abraham (1809–1865), 16th president and backwoods wit.

Lindbergh, Anne Morrow (1906–2001), American author and aviatrix; wife of Charles.

Longus (2nd century a.d.), idyllic Greek poet.

Loos, Anita (1888–1981), American novelist and humorist who definitely preferred gentlemen.

Lowry, Malcolm (1909–1957), English novelist who reflected the spiritual desolation of 20th-century man.

Luce, Clare Booth (1903–1987), witty American playwright and diplomat.

Mabley, "Moms" Jackie (1894–1975), irreverent American comic.

MacDonald, George (1824–1905), Scottish author and clergyman, known for his allegorical children's stories.

MacLaine, Shirley (b. 1934), American actress, singer, dancer, and mystic.

Mannes, Marya (1904–1990), New York–born journalist.

Mansfield, Katherine (1888–1923), British author, master of the short story.

Marcus Aurelius (121–180), stoic Roman emperor.

Marlborough, Sarah Churchill, 1st Duchess of (1660–1744), confidante of Queen Anne, ancestor of Winston Churchill.

Marlowe, Christopher (1564–1593), Elizabethan playwright and poet.

Martial (Marcus Valerius Martialis) (c. 43–104), Roman epigrammatic poet.

Marvell, Andrew (1621–1678), English metaphysical poet.

Marx, Groucho (1890–1977), irrepressible American film comedian by way of vaudeville with his four brothers, Harp, Chico, Gummo, and Zeppo.

Mason, Jackie (b. 1934), Borsht-belt stand-up comedian.

Maugham, W. Somerset (1874–1965), ironic English novelist.

Maurois, André (1885–1967), flamboyant French novelist, essayist, and biographer.

McIntyre, Vonda N. (b. 1948), American science fiction author.

Mead, Margaret (1901–1978), American sociologist and writer, best known for her work on Samoa.

Mellon, Andrew (1855–1937), American financier, industrialist, public official, and philanthropist.

Mencken, H. L. (1880–1956), American editor, author, critic, and "The Bard of Baltimore"

Menninger, Karl A. (1893–1990), American psychiatrist, co-founder of the Menninger Clinic.

Meredith, George (1828–1909), distinguished English novelist and poet.

Miss Manners (Judith Martin) (b. 1938), American columnist and etiquette expert.

Mitchell, Margaret (1900–1949), Atlanta-born novelist.

Molière, Jean-Baptiste Poquelin (1622–1673), French dramatist.

Moore, Thomas (1779–1852), English poet.

Moore, Thomas (b. 1940), lecturer and best-selling author.

Moreau, Jeanne (b. 1928), French film star whom Orson Welles called "the greatest actress in the world."

Morley, Christopher (1890–1957), American editor and author, one of the founders of the *Saturday Review of Literature.*

Mother Teresa (Agnes Gonxha Bojaxhiu) (1910–1997), Yugoslavia-born humanitarian known for her work among the poor of India.

Mozart, Wolfgang Amadeus (1756–1791), Austrian composer, child prodigy who matured into a titan of classical music.

Musset, Alfred de (1810–1857), French romantic poet, dramatist, and fiction writer.

Nathan, George Jean (1882–1958), foppish American editor and drama critic.

Nelson, Horatio (1758–1805), British admiral and national hero.

Newman, Paul (b. 1925), American movie star and entrepeneur.

Nietzsche, Friedrich (1844–1900), German philosopher.

Nixon, Pat (1912–1993), First Lady of President Richard Nixon.

O'Faoláin, Seán (1900–1991), Irish writer.

O'Rourke, P. J. (b. 1947), best-selling author, editor, and satirist.

Oates, Joyce Carol (b. 1938), American novelist.

Onassis, Jacqueline Kennedy (1929–1994), former First Lady and American icon.

Paglia, Camille (b. 1937), American writer and feminist.

Parker, Dorothy (1893–1967), American writer and humorist.

Parrish, Mary, American author on spiritual development.

Pascal, Blaise (1623–1662), French mathematician, physicist, and theologian.

Pasternak, Boris (1890–1960), Russian poet, author, and translator.

Paul, St. (c.10–65), apostle to the Gentiles and important theologian of the early Church.

Peck, M. Scott (b. 1936), best-selling American author.

Pepys, Samuel (1633–1703), famed English diarist.

Petrarch (Francesco Petrarca) (1304–1374), Italian Renaissance poet and humanist.

Philips, Emo (b. 1956), American comedian and filmmaker.

Plato (c. 427–347 B.C.), Athenian author and philosopher.

Poitier, Sidney (b. 1927), American film star; the first black man to receive an Academy Award for best actor.

Proust, Marcel (1871–1922), prolific French novelist.

Publilius Syrus (c. 1st century B.C.), Roman writer and actor.

Racine, Jean (1639–1699), French dramatist; the finest example of French Classicism.

Rawlings, Marjorie Kinnan (1896–1953), American author.

Reik, Theodor (1888–1969), American psychologist and author, an early student of Freud.

Reuben, David, M.D. (b. 1933), American physician and author.

Richardson, Samuel (1689–1761), seminal British novelist.

Rilke, Rainer Maria (1875–1926), German author.

Roberts, Nora, prolific best-selling romance author.

Rogers, Ginger (1911–1995), American stage and film actress, best known for her singing and dancing roles with Fred Astaire.

Rooney, Mickey (b. 1920), much-married American film star.

Rousseau, Jean Jacques (1712–1778), Swiss-French philosopher, author, political theorist, and composer.

Rowland, Helen (1875–1950), American writer.

Rudner, Rita (b. 1956), American stand-up comedienne/actress.

Sagan, Françoise (b. 1935), bittersweet French novelist.

Saint-Exupéry, Antoine de (1900–1944), French writer, humanistic philosopher, and aviator.

Saki (H. H. Munro) (1870–1916), a master of the short story.

Salinger, J. D. (b. 1919), American novelist, short story writer, and recluse.

Sand, Georges (1804–1876), cross-dressing French novelist.

Santayana, George (1863–1952), Spanish-born philosopher, taught at Harvard.

Sartre, Jean-Paul (1905–1980), French existential philosopher, playwright, and novelist.

Sayers, Dorothy L. (1893–1957), British mystery novelist, creator of detective Lord Peter Wimsey, and translator of Dante.

Schmidt, Gretchen entrant in San Jose State bad writing contest.

Segal, Erich (b. 1937), American novelist.

Selden, John (1584–1654), English jurist and scholar.

Shakespeare, William (1564–1616), prolific English playwright.

Shandling, Garry (b. 1949), droll American comedian and actor.

Sharp, William (Fiona Macleod) (1855–1905), Scottish poet and man of letters.

Shaw, George Bernard (1856–1950), Irish wit, playwright, and correspondent.

Shelley, Percy Bysshe (1792–1822), English romance poet.

Shore, Dinah (1917–1994), Dixie-born American songstress.

Simborg, Philip J. (b. 1944), American real estate executive.

Simpson, Wallis Warfield (1896–1986), American divorcée for whom King Edward VIII abdicated his throne.

Smith, Sydney (1771–1845), English writer, clergyman, and wit; life-long defender of the oppressed.

Smythers, Ruth, turn-of-the-century pastor's wife-turned-advice-manual author.

Socrates (469–399 B.C.), famed Greek philosopher.

Sophocles (c. 496–406 B.C.), Greek tragic poet.

Spenser, Edmund (1552–1599), Elizabethan poet.

Stead, Christina (1902–1983), Australian novelist who lived and wrote in the United States.

Steinbeck, John (1902–1968), American writer of strong psychological novels.

Steinem, Gloria (b. 1934), American feminist writer.

Stendhal (Marie-Henri Beyle) (1783–1842), one of the great French novelists.

Sterne, Laurence (1713–1768), British novelist and humorist.

Stevens, Wallace (1879–1955), American poet, master of exquisite verse.

Stevenson, Robert Louis (1850–1894), Scottish author.

Stills, Stephen (b. 1945), American folk-rock singer.

Swenson, Laura American writer.

Swinburne, Algernon Charles (1837–1909), English poet and critic, his verse is noted for its vitality.

Taylor, Elizabeth (b. 1932), much-married, violet-eyed film star.

Tennyson, Alfred, Lord (1809–1892), most famous poet of the Victorian Age.

Terence (Publius Terentius Afer) (185–159 B.C.), Carthage-born Roman writer of comedies.

Thirkell, Angela (1890–1961), charming author noted for her portrayal of English county life.

Thomas, Dylan (1914–1953), Welsh-born poet, ranked among the greatest of the 20th century.

Thomson, James (1834–1882), pessimistic Scottish poet.

Thoreau, Henry David (1817–1862), individualistic American essayist and author.

Tillett, Benjamin (1860–1943), English labor organizer.

Tillich, Paul (1886–1965), German-American theologian and philosopher of religion.

Tolstoy, Leo (1828–1910), epic Russian novelist.

Tomlin, Lily (b. 1939), irreverent American actress and comedienne.

Toscanini, Arturo (1867–1957), world-renowned Italian symphony conductor.

Tracy, Spencer (1900–1967), rugged American actor.

Trollope, Anthony (1815–1882), British novelist.

Turner, Lana (1920–1995), tempestuous American actress, known as the "Sweater Girl."

Twain, Mark (Samuel L. Clemens) (1835–1910), American humorist who had something to say on every topic.

Ustinov, Peter (b. 1921), English actor, director, and raconteur.

Van Doren, Mamie (b. 1933), South Dakota–born singer, actress, and 1950's bombshell.

Vass, Susan, American author and stand-up comedienne.

Vauvenargues, Marquis de Luc de Clapiers (1715–1747), French nobleman and writer.

Victoria (1819–1901), British monarch and definer of an age.

Villon, François (c. 1430–1465), French poet of the streets.

Viorst, Judith (b. 1931), New Jersey–born journalist, novelist, and poet.

Virgil (Publius Vergilius Maro) (70–19 B.C.), Roman writer.

Viscott, David (b. 1938), American writer on psychiatry.

Waller, Robert James (b. 1955), hugely successful romantic American novelist.

Warhol, Andy (1928–1987), enigmatic American Pop artist.

Webb, Sidney James (1859–1947), English reformer.

Webster, John (c. 1580–1634), English dramatist.

Welles, Orson (1915–1985), groundbreaking American actor, director, and producer.

Wescott, Glenway (1901–1987), Wisconsin-born novelist, essayist, and pundit.

West, Mae (1893–1980), bawdy American actress.

Wilde, Oscar (1854–1900), Irish wit, playwright, and raconteur.

Wilder, Thornton (1897–1975), American dramatist and novelist.

Wilson, Woodrow (1856–1924), 28th president.

Winfrey, Oprah (b. 1954), talk show host and one–woman industry.

Winslow, Thyra Samter (1893–1961), American writer.

Winters, Shelley (b. 1922), American actress.

Wodehouse, P. G. (1881–1975), Anglo-American novelist and humorist.

Wolfe, Thomas (1900–1938), southern author known for his mammoth autobiographical novels.

Wollstonecraft, Mary (1759–1797), British proto-feminist author; mother of Mary Shelley.

Woolf, Virginia (1882–1941), British novelist; member of the Bloomsbury group.

Wordsworth, William (1770–1850), British Lake poet.

Zangwill, Israel (1864–1926), English author and journalist.

Works Cited

Henry Brook Adams
The Education of Henry Adams (1918)

Woody Allen
Husbands and Wives (1992)

Sherwood Anderson
Winesburg, Ohio (1919)

Anonymous
Carmina Burana (c. 12th century)

St. Thomas Aquinas
Summa Theologica (1273)

Aristophanes
Lysistrata (411 B.C.)

St. Augustine
Confessions (397–401)

Jane Austen
Mansfield Park (1814)

Northanger Abbey (1818)
Persuasion (1818)
Pride and Prejudice (1813)

Honoré de Balzac
Modeste Mignon (1834)
Physiologie du mariage (1829)

J. M. Barrie
What Every Woman Knows (1908)

Lynda Barry
Big Ideas (1983)

Sir Max Beerbohm
Zuleika Dobson (1911)

George Bernanos
The Diary of a Country Priest (1936)

Elizabeth Asquith Bibesco
The Fir and the Palm (1924)

Ambrose Bierce
The Devil's Dictionary (1911)

Boethius
The Consolation of Philosophy (524)

Charlotte Brontë
Jane Eyre (1846)

Emily Brontë
Wuthering Heights (1847)

Elizabeth Barrett Browning
Sonnets from the Portuguese (1850)

Edward Robert Bulwer-Lytton
The Wanderer (1858)

Comte de Bussy-Rabutin
Histoire Amoureuse des Gaules (1665)

Nancy Butler
Prospero's Daughter (2002)

Samuel Butler
The Way of all Flesh (1903)

Lord Byron
Don Juan (1818)

Jonathan Carroll
Outside the Dog Museum (1991)

Joyce Cary
The Horse's Mouth (1944)

Miguel de Cervantes
Don Quixote (1605)

Alexander Chase
Perspectives (1966)

Raymond Chandler
Farewell, My Lovely (1940)

Geoffrey Chaucer
The Canterbury Tales (c. 1387)

Anton Pavlovich Chekhov
Complete Works and Letters in Thirty Volumes (1980)

G. K. Chesterton
Alarms and Discursions (1910)

Sandra Cisneros
The House on Mango Street (1984)

Colette
Claudine and Annie (1903)
Lettres au petit Corsaire (1963)

William Congreve
The Old Bachelor (1693)
The Way of the World (1700)

Cyril Connolly
The Unquiet Grave (1945)

Pat Conroy
The Prince of Tides (1986)

Benjamin Constant
Adolphe (1816)

Georges Courteline
La Paix Chez Soi (1903)

Clarence Day
Thoughts Without Words (1928)

Denis Diderot
Jack the Fatalist and His Master (1770)

Benjamin Disraeli
Henrietta Temple (1837)

Alexandre Dumas, père
Les Mohicans de Paris (1854–1859)

Alexandre Dumas, fils
Camille (1852)

Daphne du Maurier
Rebecca (1938)

George du Maurier
  Trilby (1894)

Marguerite Duras
  Les Petits Chevaux de Tarquinia (1953)

Havelock Ellis
  The New Spirit (1890)

Nora Ephron
  Heartburn (1983)

Nicholas Evans
  The Horse Whisperer (1995)

Henry Fairlie
  The Seven Deadly Sins Today (1978)

Helen Fielding
  Bridget Jones's Diary (1996)

F. Scott Fitzgerald
  The Last Tycoon (1941)

Gustave Flaubert
  Madame Bovary (1857)

Harry Emerson Fosdick
  Riverside Sermons (1958)

Gene Fowler
   Skyline (1961)

Anatole France
   The Garden of Epicurus (1894)

Sigmund Freud
   Civilization and Its Discontents (1930)

Erich Fromm
   The Art of Loving (1956)

Margaret Fuller
   Summer on the Lakes (1844)

John Galsworthy
   The Man of Property (1906)

John Gay
   The Beggar's Opera (1728)

Kahlil Gibran
   The Prophet (1923)

Sir William S. Gilbert
   Iolanthe (1882)

Jean Giraudoux
   Amphityron (1929)

Emma Goldman
Anarchism and Other Essays (1910)

William Goldman
The Princess Bride (1973)

E. and J. De Goncourt
Journal (1891)

Maxim Gorky
The Lower Depths (1902)

C. H. Grattan
Bitter Bierce (1929)

John Gray, Ph.D.
Men Are from Mars, Women Are from Venus (1992)

Germaine Greer
The Female Eunuch (1970)

Matt Groening
Love is Hell (1985)

Sacha Guitry
Elles et toi (1948)

Dafydd ap Gwilym
Plygu rhag ilid yr ydwyf (c. 14th century)

Elizabeth Hardwick
   Seduction and Betrayal (1974)

Robert Heinlein
   Time Enough for Love (1973)

Joseph Heller
   Something Happened (1974)

Ernest Hemingway
   For Whom the Bell Tolls (1940)

O. Henry
   The Four Million (1906)

James Hilton
   Random Harvest (1941)

Alice Hoffman
   Practical Magic (1995)

Lady Holland
   *A Memoir of Reverend Sydney Holland by His Daughter,
   Lady Holland* (1855)

Nick Hornby
   About a Boy (1998)
   High Fidelity (1995)

Barbara Howar
Laughing All the Way (1973)

Edgar Watson Howe
Country Town Sayings (1911)

Victor Hugo
Les Miserables (1862)

Morton Hunt
The Natural History of Love (1959)

Aldous Huxley
Antic Hay (1923)
Eyeless in Gaza (1936)

Henrik Ibsen
A Doll's House (1879)

Washington Irving
Bracebridge Hall (1822)

Henry James
The Portrait of a Lady (1881)

Jerome K. Jerome
The Idle Thoughts of an Idle Fellow (1886)

Douglas Jerrold
The Wit and Opinions of Douglas Jerrold (1859)

John Keats
You Might as Well Live: The Life and Times of Dorothy Parker (1970)

Ann Landers
Truth Is Stranger (1968)

Lao-tzu
Tao te Ching (550 B.C.)

Francois, 7th duc de La Rochefoucauld
Maxims (1665)
Reflections (1665)

John Le Carré
A Perfect Spy (1986)

Doris Lessing
The Golden Notebook (1962)

Anne Morrow Lindbergh
Locked Rooms and Open Doors (1974)

Longus
Daphnis and Chloe (2nd century)

Anita Loos
  Gentlemen Prefer Blondes (1925)

Marya Mannes
  More in Anger (1958)

Christopher Marlowe
  Dr. Faustus (c. 1588)

Martial
  Epigrammata (c. 64)

W. Somerset Maugham
  The Bread-Winner (1930)
  Lady Frederick (1907)
  The Summing Up (1938)

Vonda N. McIntyre
  The Moon and the Sun (1997)

H. L. Mencken
  Prejudices (1919–1927)

Karl A. Menninger
  Sparks (1973)

George Meredith
  The Ordeal of Richard Feverel (1859)

Margaret Mitchell
   Gone With the Wind (1936)

Thomas Moore
   Care of the Soul (1992)

Christopher Morley
   Kitty Foyle (1939)

George Jean Nathan
   The Theater, the Drama and the Girls (1921)

Blaise Pascal
   Pensées (1660)

Boris Pasternak
   Dr. Zhivago (1957)

M. Scott Peck
   The Road Less Traveled (1978)

Samuel Pepys
   Diary (published 1825)

Marcel Proust
   Remembrance of Things Past: Cities of the Plain (1922)

Publilius Syrus
   Maxim (42 B.C.)

Jean Racine
Andromache (1667)

Marjorie Kinnan Rawlings
The Yearling (1938)

Theodor Reik
Of Love and Lust (1957)

David Reuben, M.D.
Everything You Ever Wanted to Know About Sex (1969)

Samuel Richardson
Clarissa (1747)

Nora Roberts
Without a Trace (1990)

Helen Rowland
Reflections of a Bachelor Girl (1903)
A Guide to Men (1922)

Françoise Sagan
Le Soir (1960)

Saki
Beasts and Super-Beasts (1914)

J. D. Salinger
The Catcher in the Rye (1951)

George Santayana
The Life of Reason: Reason in Society (1906)

Dorothy L. Sayers
Gaudy Night (1935)

Erich Segal
Love Story (1970)

John Selden
Table Talk (1689)

William Shakespeare
Antony and Cleopatra (c. 1606)
As You Like It (c. 1599)
Hamlet (1603)
A Midsummer Night's Dream (c. 1595)
Much Ado About Nothing (c. 1598)
Romeo and Juliet (1597)
The Two Gentlemen of Verona (1594)

George Bernard Shaw
John Bull's Other Island (1907)
Man and Superman (1905)
Pygmalion (1913)

Ruth Smythers
Marriage Advice for Women (1894)

Edmund Spenser
Epithalamion (1595)
The Faerie Queen (1500–1596)

Antoine de St.-Exupéry
Wind, Sand and Stars (1939)

Christina Stead
For Love Alone (1944)

Stendhal
De l'amour (1822)

Laurence Sterne
Tristram Shandy (1759–67)

Wallace Stevens
Wallace Stevens: A Celebration (1980)

Robert Louis Stevenson
Virginibus Puerisque (1881)

Terence
Andria (c. 66 B.C.)

Angela Thirkell
Cheerfulness Breaks In (1941)

Leo Tolstoy
Anna Karenina (1875–1877)
War and Peace (1865–1869)

Anthony Trollope
The Way We Live Now (1875)

Mark Twain
Following the Equator (1897)

Virgil
Aeneid (19 B.C.)

David Viscott
How to Live with Another Person (1974)

Robert James Waller
The Bridges of Madison County (1992)

Andy Warhol
Andy Warhol's Exposures (1979)
From A to B and Back Again (1975)

John Webster
The Duchess of Malfi (1614)

Oscar Wilde
   An Ideal Husband (c. 1895)
   The Importance of Being Ernest (1895)
   The Picture of Dorian Gray (1890)
   A Woman of No Importance (1893)

P. G. Wodehouse
   Much Obliged, Jeeves (1971)
   Summer Lightning (1929)

Thomas Wolfe
   Of Time and the River (1935)

Mary Wollstonecraft
   A Vindication of the Rights of Women (1792)

Virginia Woolf
   A Room of One's Own (1929)
   To the Lighthouse (1927)

Index